AN EMPTY CURRICULUM

AN EMPTY CURRICULUM

The Need to Reform Teacher Licensing Regulations and Tests

Sandra Stotsky

ROWMAN & LITTLEFIELD
Lanham • Boulder • New York • London

Published by Rowman & Littlefield
A wholly owned subsidiary of The Rowman & Littlefield Publishing Group,
Inc.
4501 Forbes Boulevard, Suite 200, Lanham, Maryland 20706
www.rowman.com

Unit A, Whitacre Mews, 26-34 Stannary Street, London SE11 4AB

British Library Cataloguing in Publication Information Available

Library of Congress Cataloging-in-Publication Data Available

ISBN 978-1-4758-1566-5 (cloth : alk. paper)
ISBN 978-1-4758-1567-2 (paper : alk. paper)
ISBN 978-1-4758-1568-9 (electronic)

♾™ The paper used in this publication meets the minimum requirements of
American National Standard for Information Sciences Permanence of Paper
for Printed Library Materials, ANSI/NISO Z39.48-1992.

Printed in the United States of America

CONTENTS

PREFACE: WHAT LED TO THE "MASSACHUSETTS EDUCATION MIRACLE"?

Most governors, state commissioners of education, state boards of education, and chambers of commerce seem to have an unshakable confidence in Common Core's standards as the silver bullet that will make all K–12 students college and career ready. This confidence is remarkable for two reasons. First, Common Core's standards are vastly different from those in the one state—Massachusetts—whose pre–Common Core standards led to greatly increased student achievement in reading, mathematics, and science in its common public schools and in its vocational/technical high schools.[1] Second, it is not at all clear that the Bay State's standards, however superior they were to Common Core's, were the decisive factor responsible for the "Massachusetts education miracle."

The gains were deservedly noteworthy, putting the Bay State in first place on five consecutive National Assessment of Educational Progress (NAEP) tests in both grade 4 and grade 8, in both reading and mathematics, and from 2005 to 2013. Moreover, international tests confirmed these gains. Bay State students were in a first-place tie in grade 8 science and among the top countries in grade 8 mathematics on Trends in International Mathematics and Science Study (TIMSS) in 2007 and 2011 (the state had entered as a separate country). In addition, most Bay State regional vocational/technical high schools (all with grades 9–12) now have high pass rates in mathematics and English on the state's high school tests, an attrition rate that is close to zero, and long waiting lists.

It is true that the Bay State's standards in all major subjects had also been rated by independent academic experts as among the best sets of state standards long before Common Core came into being. But as the person often cited as the driver behind its first-class standards, I have been trying for five years to inform reporters and education researchers that these standards do not by themselves necessarily account for the gains in achievement by all demographic groups and by our regional vocational/technical high schools (which enroll a disproportionate number of special education students and below-grade-level readers). Other important policies were put into place at the very same time. Some helped to strengthen the academic knowledge and skills of the state's teaching corps, wherever they taught. Others affected other aspects of K–12 education.

However, without the changes Massachusetts made to its entire system of teacher licensing (e.g., subject area licensing tests for all prospective teachers, criteria for achieving full licensure after beginning teaching, and criteria for license renewal for veteran teachers), it is unlikely there would have been enduring gains in achievement for students in all demographic groups and in all its regional vocational/technical high schools—gains confirmed by tests independent of control or manipulation by Massachusetts or federal policy makers.

No other state did what Massachusetts did—that is, redo almost every aspect of its licensing system. The state's K–12 standards used for teaching, testing, and professional development were being revised and strengthened at the same time as its licensing system was being revised. As a result, it has been difficult for observers to determine which factor or group of factors was most responsible for these gains: a revised and strengthened licensing system; revised or new licensure tests; the use of first-rate standards in most classrooms, in annual state student tests, and in the professional development programs all teachers took for license renewal; and/or the major changes in K–12 governance and finance introduced by the Massachusetts Education Reform Act of 1993.

Nevertheless, this book seeks to make the case, with empirical support wherever possible, that the revision of the licensing system for each stage in a teaching career and the construction of new or more demanding teacher licensure tests contributed significantly to the long-lasting effects of the state's first-class standards. A rethought licensing system came into being in 2000, followed by new criteria for license renewal and new or revised licensing tests in the next few years, just as the state's K–12 standards were being revised in mathematics, science, English, reading, history, geography, economics, and U.S. government. A few changes in licensing requirements, in license renewal, and in one licensing test have been made since then; otherwise, the same system has been in place for over a decade.

I was put in complete charge of the revision of the Bay State's licensing regulations and teacher licensure tests in the summer of 1999. While most of my work concerned regulations and tests for teachers of "academic" subjects, I also helped to revise licensing regulations for teachers of "shop" courses in vocational/technical high schools in Massachusetts, and thereby learned about the differences in the licensing systems for these two types of teachers.

At the time I was hired (in the spring of 1999) as a senior staff member in the Massachusetts Department of Elementary and Secondary Education (DESE), my first major assignment was the immediate and total revision of the state's almost incomprehensible 1994 licensing regulations. Revision of these regulations led to revision of many of the 41 subject area licensure tests that had been constructed in 1995–1998 in response to requirements in the Massachusetts Education Reform Act (MERA) of 1993.

This model piece of legislation, written chiefly by the state's governor, Senate president, and House Education Committee chair, sought three goals relating to teacher quality and the supply of teachers: to attract more high-achieving undergraduate majors, college graduates, and midcareer changers to teaching as a career; to increase the academic qualifications of those entering the profession; and to increase the academic knowledge of the teaching force itself. Strengthening the state's teacher corps was one of MERA's central objectives. In the legislature's view, student achievement could not be increased without strengthening teachers' academic background.

Revised regulations as well as revised or newly created licensure tests were needed to make sure that new teachers as well as those already teaching could teach to the stronger academic content in the K–12 standards that I had also been asked to revise. I was, in effect, master controller for a number of planes that all had to take off at once. Revised K–12 standards were to be used immediately for student tests that would be used to judge school performance, while revised regulations were to serve as the basis for teacher training programs, teacher licensing tests, and teacher professional development to enable all teachers to teach to these revised K–12 standards.

Besides the charge to revise the state's regulations for "program approval" and teacher licensure, I was also given the testing company to work with in order to revise the relatively new subject area licensure tests developed from 1995–1998. National Evaluation Systems (NES) had won the contract in 1994–1995 to develop both a generic teacher skills test and the 41 subject area licensing tests required by MERA (no tests of pedagogy were required), and its contract had been renewed at about the time I began work in the department. My signature was required for every step in test development (spelled out in test specifications approved by the commissioner of education), so I participated in every phase of test development to the extent I could. I wanted to understand the procedures for developing licensure tests as well as the dynamics of meetings for classroom teachers, college education faculty, and college arts and sciences faculty. Members of these three groups were all required by test specifications to review test objectives and test items and to set a pass score on teacher licensure tests.

Teachers cannot teach what they do not know. In the past half century, this country has tolerated a weak licensing system for prospective teachers. This weak system has been accompanied by an increasingly emptier curriculum for most of our students, depriving them of the knowledge and skills they need for this country's experiment in self-government and for their careers in a highly industrialized state. An academically stronger licensing system for teachers would raise the academic quality of our teaching force, strengthen the school curriculum, and, in turn, increase student achievement.

One purpose of this book is to explain what my staff and I did in 2000 to strengthen the state's licensure system for teachers in both regular and vocational/technical programs in order to ensure that all teachers could teach to relatively strong K–12 standards. In other words, I explain what contributed (significantly, in my judgment) to the Massachusetts "education miracle." Its larger purpose is to suggest that while the first step in strengthening public education in this country is the development of strong academic standards in all major subjects, the second should be a complete revision (or tightening up of the academic screws, so to speak) of a state's teacher licensing system, not, as has been the case for several decades, the development of statewide or nationwide K–12 student tests.

NOTE

1. Despite the nationally recognized quality of the state's English, mathematics, and science standards, the state's Board of Elementary and Secondary Education replaced them with Common Core's English and mathematics standards in July 2010 for the guarantee of $250,000,000 of Race to the Top funds. In addition, the Department of Elementary and Secondary Education in 2014 is quietly replacing the state's first-class science standards with Achieve, Inc.'s Next Generation Science Standards (which are aligned to Common Core's) before the Board officially votes in 2015 to junk the state's science standards, too. Why it is doing so is as unknown to the public as are its intentions.

I

WHY WE KNOW SO LITTLE ABOUT TEACHER LICENSURE TESTS

This chapter notes why we know so little about teacher licensure tests. It describes the major sources of information drawn on for this book and offers definitions of key terms.

PROBLEM

One of the several licensure tests all prospective teachers in the United States must pass in order to receive a teaching license purports to assess their knowledge of the subject(s) they plan to teach. State policy makers seem to believe that simply requiring prospective teachers to pass a test claiming to assess their knowledge of the subjects they will teach solved the century-long problem of how to assure parents that their children's teachers were academically competent to teach the subjects they were legally licensed to teach. Unfortunately, this belief is based on a myth, with unintended negative consequences for every subject in the school curriculum.

Above all, the myth has served as a pillar sustaining the rickety pantheon of so-called "teacher education reforms" in this country. These putative reforms (like lengthening the number of weeks for student teaching, or eliminating licensure tests altogether) address almost everything except ways to strengthen the tests that were designed to assure the public that new teachers have a firm grasp of what they are licensed to teach even if they don't yet know how to teach it well. The cold truth is that most subject area tests at present do not, and cannot, guarantee aspiring teachers' academic competence in the subject(s) they will teach—no matter where the pass score is set.

At a time when the phrase "teacher quality" is on the lips of almost every education policy maker as a goal devoutly to be desired, it is puzzling why so few researchers have examined what is on subject area licensure tests for teachers and why. Less than a handful of studies have sought to find out if in fact they assess important topics in the subject(s) they claim to measure and, if they do, the extent to which they do. We have almost no information independent of the test makers themselves on whether the content of teacher licensure tests addresses what prospective teachers should have been taught in their academic courses, given the range of grade levels and students they will be licensed to teach and the curriculum content they will be expected to teach.

Why should licensure tests for prospective teachers (whether of their academic knowledge or their pedagogical approach) be any different from state tests of K–12 students? There are few, if any, studies of the match between what students were taught in their classrooms and what was on the state tests they took. While prospective teachers should expect their academic and education coursework to prepare them for passing their licensure tests, when they do pass (as most do), we do not know if their coursework prepared them to pass, if the passing score is set so low that most test takers pass no matter what is on the test, or if the test contained the right material for the range of grade levels and students covered by the license. Even if the pass score is set high and many test takers fail the test, we still don't know if the test contained the "right" stuff or why test takers failed.

In one sense it is puzzling why there are so few studies on the content of teacher licensure tests and on how, if at all, teacher tests are related to test takers' teacher preparation programs and the arts and sciences courses they took. In another sense the paucity of research on licensure tests by educational researchers in education schools is not at all puzzling. The few curious reporters and educators who have examined the sample test items for a test[1] or taken a licensure test to find out what was on it[2] have reported being aghast at the low level of difficulty of teachers' skills test and at the failure of tests for prospective elementary teachers to reflect (and therefore drive) evidence-based instructional practices. Why would researchers want to provide documentation for consistently negative anecdotes when colleagues at their education schools may have served as advisors to the test companies providing these licensure tests?

Today there is an additional problem. Let us assume that subject area licensure tests don't assess adequately the background knowledge prospective teachers need for teaching to the state's content standards at the grade levels covered by the license they seek and to the range of students apt to be at these grade levels. Do test inadequacies reflect the limitations of these prospective teachers' academic coursework, or do they reflect simply low expectations by test developers and their consultants? If licensure tests reflect less demanding coursework, not just low expectations, teachers' lack of academic knowledge logically should influence what their students learn. But will the right parties be held accountable?

For example, elementary teachers have likely not majored or minored in science or mathematics and have not been expected in education methods courses to show deep conceptual understanding of the mathematics content they will teach future students. If their students get low scores on their mathematics tests, is the problem the tests, student effort and ability, and/or teachers' academic competence? If their licensure tests had low academic demands and/or low pass scores, school administrators cannot be sure their teachers knew enough to teach the content of the curriculum.

Yet, teachers will be held accountable to some extent for student scores on Common Core–based tests, not the instructors of their academic and education coursework who were responsible for preparing them to be competent teachers. Nor will test developers, the state board, commissioner of education, department of education staff, and consultants from the education schools be held accountable, even though all of them played a role in shaping the content of the tests the teachers had to have passed in order to get a license to teach.

K–8 teachers will try to teach their students whatever they think Common Core–based tests assess, as well as how to respond to the question types on the tests. If teachers want their students to do well on these tests, much class time will be spent "teaching to the tests." Inasmuch as teachers, not their students, will be held accountable for the students' scores on Common Core–based tests, we can expect a great deal more time spent on teaching to the tests, whether or not they are worth teaching to. But without any accountability for those who taught these teachers and shaped their licensure tests, it seems unfair to hold only teachers accountable for the test scores of those they are now teaching. The academic level of most subject area licensure tests for elementary and middle school teachers is so low, we don't know whether teacher education faculty simply didn't teach to these tests because their pass scores are also low, or deliberately shaped them so that they reflect or reinforce what they choose to teach prospective teachers.

SOURCES OF INFORMATION

This book draws on several sources of information. First, the websites for the major organizations that develop teacher tests: Educational Testing Service (ETS), Evaluation Systems of Pearson (formerly National Evaluation Systems, NES), and the American Board for the Certification of Teacher Excellence (ABCTE). Organizations that offer teacher tests provide on their websites detailed outlines of the standards or competencies on which their tests are based, an overview of the major categories on each test, the weights for each category, and sample items for each category, whether multiple-choice or essay prompts. They also provide practice tests for high-incidence licensure tests. A wealth of information can be mined from a perusal of these materials alone.

Second, the observations from staff members in departments of education and from education school faculty in several states on their perceptions of the influence of teacher testing on their preparation programs and on the arts and sciences coursework taken by prospective teachers.

Third, my experiences at the Massachusetts Department of Education from 1999 to 2003, where I was in charge of revising the state's K–12 standards in every basic subject, its regulations for approving teacher and administrator preparation programs, and its licensure tests for teachers in both the regular public schools and its vocational/technical high schools. Almost all the state's subject tests for teachers needed to be revised after passage in 2000 of new regulations for licensing teachers, and I worked closely with National Evaluation Systems, the organization that had won the contract to develop the state's tests in the mid-1990s, on every phase of test development for revising or creating over 20 major subject area tests, largely because of new and clearer academic requirements in the state's new licensing regulations. I was also able to learn a great deal from several nationally recognized experts in large-scale assessment and in the development of professional licensure tests who evaluated the soundness of the state's teacher testing program in 2002 as required by the legislature.

Finally, the historical, descriptive, and experimental research on licensure tests for teachers. I review research on the predictive validity of licensure tests for student achievement; surveys of requirements for teacher licensure internationally and in other professions; and research on the content or other aspects of teacher licensure tests.

DEFINITIONS OF KEY TERMS

A *certificate* is awarded by a nongovernmental agency or association to an individual who has met the requirements specified by the agency or association usually by means of a particular course of studies. For example, the National Board for Professional Teaching Standards awards a certificate to those who complete its program. Teachers' licenses have often been called "certificates" because the process for obtaining a license has traditionally been called "certification," but they are in fact licenses because they are awarded by the state.

A *license* is a permit granted by a governmental agency to an individual who has met specified requirements. A teacher training institution cannot grant a license. At the most, the institution may recommend a candidate for licensure who has fulfilled the specified training requirements it has provided. Teachers must obtain a license to teach in a public school in every state (unless otherwise allowed for public charter schools), although they need not complete an "approved program," traditional or alternative, in order to obtain a license. A license for professional practice (as in medicine, law, clinical psychology, or teaching) provides some measure of quality control and consumer protection at the individual level.

Program approval is a process in which peer review of program coursework and a site visit by a team of peers determine whether a teacher training program meets state regulatory requirements and can make recommendations for licensure. A state department of education may provide its own review teams (as Massachusetts does for most licensure programs in the state) to make recommendations for "program approval." Or a nongovernmental agency such as the Council for the Accreditation of Educator Preparation (CAEP), a merger of the National Council for Accreditation of Teacher Education (NCATE) and the Teacher Education Accreditation Council (TEAC), may also review program coursework (for a fee) and make a site visit in order to recommend "program approval" to the state agency awarding licenses. Program approval, or accreditation as it may also be called, provides consumer protection and quality control at the institutional level in pre-service preparation.

Licensure tests are tests that have been developed and/or approved by a state agency to assess prospective teachers' basic qualifications for licensure in that state. As is true of licensure tests for other professions, they are not under the control of the preparation programs themselves, although they are heavily influenced by them. They are not intended to serve as achievement, intelligence, or diagnostic tests. They sample from many (presumably relevant) domains and determine whether the test taker has what has been judged entry-level knowledge for independent practice as "teacher of record."

Most important to understand, compensatory scoring is used to arrive at a raw score (the total number of items correct across all sections of a test), which is then translated into a scaled score. Depending on where the pass score is set, test takers can conceivably fail whole sections of a test but still pass the test as a whole. As with most other licensure tests, the test taker either passes or fails; test takers who fail may retake a test as many times as they wish (and many do).

POINTS TO REMEMBER

1. Most licensure tests of prospective teachers' academic knowledge do not ensure that licensed teachers know enough about the subjects they teach in order to teach their content to the range of grades or students they are legally licensed to teach.

2. There is little research on the academic demands and quality of teacher licensure tests, so the public knows almost nothing about their contents and quality.

3. Teachers' lack of adequate academic knowledge of the subjects they teach logically influences the curriculum they can teach and what their students can learn.

4. It is not clear why teachers should be held accountable for student achievement on a Common Core–based test even though their state's preparation programs, commissioner of education, state department of education, and state board of education are responsible for the low academic level of teachers' licensure tests and their lack of adequate knowledge of the subjects they teach.

NOTES

1. See Melanie Scarborough, "More Than Money for Teachers," *The Washington Post*, Tuesday, July 17, 2001, A 17. http://www.washingtonpost.com/ac2wp-dyn/A6399-2001jul16?language-printer. Based on an examination of sample test items, this reporter judged that PRAXIS I was not even at a high school level of difficulty.

2. See the comprehensive report on teacher education by George K. Cunningham, formerly a professor of special education at the University of Louisville. http://www.johnlocke.org/acrobat/articles/cunninghameducationschools.pdf. In a personal note to me (undated), he commented on the PRAXIS I test he had taken to understand what his students were expected to know in order to pass the test. His report includes a discussion of teacher licensing tests.

2

WHO NEEDS A LICENSE TO TEACH AND WHY?

For many years, prospective teachers for public schools in this country were awarded a teaching certificate, often for a lifetime, if they were deemed to have met local or state requirements. Lifetime certificates are no longer awarded by any state. Once states began to require prospective teachers to pass a state-authorized test before they could be hired by a public school in the state and to earn a specified number of professional development credits in a specified cycle of years to continue teaching, it became more accurate to say that teachers were being awarded a license or a renewed license, not a certificate. However, not all K–12 teachers need a license. This chapter reviews the purpose of a professional license and who is required to hold a license in order to teach.

PURPOSE FOR LICENSURE IN OTHER PROFESSIONS

Licensure tests are the key measure of quality control for entry into most professions in this country. They are obstacles deliberately placed in the path of anyone who wants to practice the profession. In order to take a licensure test, aspiring professionals are usually required to complete the preparation program leading to licensure or to satisfy the requirements for licensure in other ways. But, it is important to note that taking a licensure test is not a one-time matter. For many, perhaps most, professions—law, for example—test takers may retake a licensure test they have failed more than once until they pass it.

Most licensure tests require aspiring members of the profession to demonstrate "entry-level knowledge and skills" for practicing the profession. For example, certified public accountants (CPAs) are the only licensed accounting professionals in the United States and have passed the Uniform CPA Examination to become a professional accountant. The purpose statement for this examination reads as follows:

> The purpose of the Uniform CPA Examination is to provide reasonable assurance to Boards of Accountancy (the state entities that have statutory authority to issue licenses) that those who pass the CPA Examination possess the level of technical knowledge and the skills necessary for initial licensure in protection of the public interest. Public interest is protected when only qualified individuals are admitted into the profession.[1]

Similarly, the purpose of the United States Medical Licensure Examination is to assess "a physician's ability to apply knowledge, concepts, and principles, and to demonstrate fundamental patient-centered skills that are important in health and disease and that constitute the basis of safe and effective patient care."[2] The importance of this particular licensure exam in upgrading the quality of the average physician in this country was underscored in a commentary on American medical education in the early decades of the twentieth century. As the author, Robert Hampel, commented: The "few innovations occurred before and after, not during, medical education. Selective admissions, rare before the 1920s, eliminated the unqualified, as did tougher state licensing exams."[3] These two types of quality control—selective admissions and tough licensing exams—still serve to maintain the quality of medical school graduates in this country—and medical care. The absence of these two types of quality control for prospective teachers helps to explain why this country does not have a highly respected teaching force and a strong public school system.

PURPOSE FOR LICENSURE FOR TEACHERS IN PUBLIC SCHOOLS

The two major reasons for the development of teacher licensure tests are: to protect the public (as with most, if not all, licenses) and to make teacher training programs accountable for the initial academic competence of those who complete their programs. There is now a growing movement to hold teacher training programs accountable for the initial pedagogical competence of their graduates as well, although it is not clear how a performance assessment at the completion of student teaching by program faculty can be monitored by an external, independent agency.

Interestingly, licensure tests in other professions have not typically been motivated by legislators' interest in making their professional training programs accountable for graduates' performance on these tests (e.g., law schools are generally not held accountable by the state in which they are located for their graduates' pass rates on the state's bar exam). However, this has been a major reason for these tests for prospective teachers since the 1990s. Massachusetts legislators, for example, explicitly mandated written tests of teachers' academic skills and content knowledge in the Massachusetts Education Reform Act of 1993 to assure a minimal level of academic competence in new teachers *and* also to make their preparation programs accountable. Similarly motivated, a provision in Title II of the 1998 and 2008 reauthorizations of the Higher Education Act (HEA) required each state to report annually on the pass rates for prospective teachers in licensure programs at each of their own institutions of higher education.

WHY TEACHERS IN PRIVATE SCHOOLS DON'T NEED A LICENSE

Historically, teachers in private schools have never been required by the state to be licensed (or certified). The reason often given is that private schools are not subject to state authority. However, private schools are subject to some state requirements in order to be chartered. Thus, a better answer is that parents place their children in private schools as an optional alternative to a public school and it is their responsibility to make sure their children's teachers are satisfactory.

Nevertheless, many elementary and special education teachers in private schools are expected by their school to hold a teaching license even if not required by the state to do so, and many faith-based private school systems require their teachers to hold a certificate from their own faith-based teacher training programs. So some credentialing is seen as desirable by some private schools for some teaching positions. On the other hand, many private schools regularly hire as teachers people with only a liberal arts undergraduate degree or a graduate degree in a discipline and do not require applicants to have completed a licensure program in an education school or to have taken any education courses at all.

WHY ALL TEACHERS IN CHARTER SCHOOLS DON'T NEED A LICENSE

Charter schools are public schools that generally operate independently of traditional school districts. Since 1992, they have grown in number from one in Minnesota to about 5,000 in 40 states and the District of Columbia. (Ten states don't have laws allowing charter schools.) In many states, charter schools are not required to hire licensed teachers (e.g., Arizona, District of Columbia, Georgia, and Texas). In some states (e.g., Illinois, Louisiana, and New Hampshire), charter schools are required to employ a given percentage of licensed teachers; the others may be unlicensed.[4] In Massachusetts, charter schools are not required to hire licensed teachers, but prospective teachers must pass the subject area licensure test for the subject they teach.

POINTS TO REMEMBER

1. Members of most professions today must pass a state-specific licensure test to enter and practice the profession.
2. The purpose of most licensure tests is to protect the public. There is a dual purpose for teacher's licensure tests: to protect children from incompetent teachers and to make prospective

teachers' preparation programs accountable for producing competent teachers.

3. Only teachers in traditional public schools need a license to teach. They don't need a teaching license in order to work in most private schools and in many states' charter schools.

NOTES

1. "The Uniform CPA Examination: Purpose and Structure," American Institute of Certified Public Accountants. http://www.aicpa.org/becomeacpa/ cpaexam/examoverview/purposeandstructure/pages/default.aspx.

2. "United States Medical Licensing Examination," ISMLE. http://www. usmle.org/.

3. Robert L. Hampel, "Doctoring Schools," Commentary, *Education Week,* October 19, 2005. www.udel.edu/soe/hampel/dschool.html.

4. "Charter School Teacher Certification," mb2.ecs.org (Model Builder: Education Commission of the States). http://mb2.ecs.org/reports/Report.aspx? id=93.

3

ABOUT TEACHER LICENSURE TESTS

Licensure tests for teachers are not intended to serve as achievement tests, diagnostic tests, or intelligence tests. Teacher licensure tests are constructed to serve their own distinctive purposes. This chapter describes the organizations that develop teacher licensure tests, types of licensure tests, how they differ from licensure tests given for other professions, the meaning of their pass scores, and what we know about them from research studies.

ORGANIZATIONS THAT DEVELOP TEACHER LICENSURE TESTS

Two private testing companies develop most of the teacher tests used by the states. Educational Testing Service (ETS) provides licensure tests for over 35 states, chiefly states with small populations, while Evaluation Systems group of Pearson (formerly National Evaluation Systems or NES) contracts to provide tailor-made tests for over 12 states, chiefly the most populous states (e.g., California, Georgia, Illinois, Minnesota, New York, and Texas). Over 50 percent of U.S. teachers were licensed in NES states at the time of Mitchell and Barth's 1999 study (discussed below).

Established in 2001, the American Board for Certification of Teacher Excellence (ABCTE) is a new player on the scene. Its online programs and tests are designed for prospective teachers who do not wish to enroll in a traditional preparation program, for current teachers seeking additional licenses or endorsements, and for current teachers seeking master teacher status. At present, aspiring teachers in nine states can use ABCTE's programs and tests to achieve full licensure.

TYPES OF TEACHER LICENSURE TESTS

There are four different types of licensure tests prospective teachers may be required to take: (1) a test of their reading, writing, and arithmetic skills; (2) a test of their knowledge of the subject(s) they seek a license to teach; (3) a test of their knowledge of the characteristics of a particular population of students they will be licensed to teach, as well as the professional issues that must be addressed in educating this population; and (4) a test of their knowledge of the pedagogical theories and strategies that are taught to prospective teachers in their preparation programs and in much of their professional development. These four types of tests assess very different things. Yet (3) is considered a "subject area" test and in some states is the only subject area test required of prospective special education teachers, even though tests of professional knowledge assess no subject area knowledge, and special education teachers most often teach children whose chief problems lie in reading, writing, and mathematics.

LEGAL BASIS FOR TEACHER LICENSURE TESTS

ETS tests are off-the-shelf tests and are therefore not based on any one state's specific standards. They were developed with the help, chiefly, of professional organizations for teachers and consultants from education schools.

ABCTE's tests are also not based on any one state's standards. They were developed with the help of a range of educators and discipline-based experts.

On the other hand, NES tests must be based on—or closely related to—a state's K–12 standards. That is one major reason why states contract with NES for their licensure tests. They want teacher tests that address the standards they are to teach to.

There is value in having teacher tests tailored to a state's own standards if the standards are academically strong. There is also value in using educators in the state's schools and its institutions of higher education to review test objectives and test items. Use of local educators ensures that the items are relevant to the academic standards that teachers must teach to in the grades covered by the license they seek.

On the other hand, if a state's standards are academically weak, then teacher tests embedding them will further damage an already damaged school curriculum. And if those who review test items do not themselves teach academically demanding courses, they are unlikely to approve of test items that reflect content they do not teach.

WHEN TEACHER LICENSURE TESTS ARE TAKEN

For initial licensure, almost all states require a test assessing a teaching candidate's basic reading, writing, and arithmetic skills, as well as a subject area test. Sometimes more than one subject area test is required. These tests are taken at different junctures in teacher preparation but typically *not* at the completion of the program, unlike most professional licensure tests. Budding social workers, librarians, doctors, lawyers, and other professionals take their licensure tests after they complete their professional training program and are generally not allowed to take them before they complete the program.

Because many, if not most, states do not mandate when teacher licensure tests are to be taken, a growing number of teacher training institutions use the skills test to screen admission *into* their licensure programs. In states contracting with ETS, the PRAXIS I test is used for this purpose. In states contracting with NES, a skills test developed by NES for this purpose is used by the state. The subject area test, which often includes items on teaching methods, is increasingly being used to screen admission *into student teaching in undergraduate licensure programs.* However, both types of tests are usually required for admission *into postbaccalaureate programs* for the initial license. College graduates who want to become teachers via a postbaccalaureate program (e.g., an M.Ed. program) for a core subject, but cannot pass the subject area test, may be admitted conditionally until they pass it—certainly before they are allowed to do student teaching.

Different academic problems flow from an institution's requirement that undergraduates pass the state's subject area test before doing student teaching, typically in the senior year. If they take and pass the test at the end of their junior year, they may not take any more upper level courses in their major or in other areas if they have already satisfied the requirements for the major. On the other hand, college graduates who apply for admission to a postbaccalaureate licensure program and must pass the relevant subject area test for admission are not necessarily required to have majored or minored in the subject they want to teach. (For example, a college graduate who majored in psychology could apply for a postbaccalaureate teacher preparation program in history and pass the history licensure test for admission. A relatively low passing score makes such an anomaly possible.)

Either of these chronological sequences for taking a licensure test makes no sense in other professions, chiefly because the *academic content* in their training programs is specific to the profession whether the program is at the postbaccalaureate level (e.g., law, library science, medicine, or social work) or at the undergraduate level (e.g., engineering). A licensure test of that academic content could not logically precede students' admission to a program or be taken part way through one.

MEANING OF PASS SCORES

We do not know what a passing score on a teacher licensure test means academically. There are several reasons for our state of ignorance.

First, we do not know much if anything about the content of most tests. Unlike state tests for K–12 students whose common items are released every year if statutorily mandated, licensure tests must be kept secure so that the same test can be used in many administrations of the test over a period of years. (A small pool of highly similar essay questions for the Open Response test items may be systematically rotated from one test administration to another to prevent cheating, i.e., to prevent a test taker from memorizing the essay questions used in one test administration and then passing the questions along to a test taker taking a later administration of the test.) Because there has been almost no research on the quality of the content on these tests and their difficulty level (in large part because researchers do not have access to them for these purposes), we cannot know what level of difficulty, or command of disciplinary content, its pass score reflects.

Second, compensatory scoring is used for most ETS and NES tests and for ABCTE tests, meaning that a test taker's raw score is the total number of items answered correctly, not a weighted number depending on the number of items answered correctly in each section of the test. As a consequence, a test taker can miss part or all of an important section on a test and still pass (and get a license to teach). This is especially important for "multi-subject" tests, tests that assess knowledge of the several subjects the license allows the teacher to teach (as in an elementary general curriculum test).

Third, pass scores do not provide comparable information on academic competence for a specific field across tests developed by different testing companies or across states on the same test. Each ETS state determines its own pass score, which may differ from that of another state using the same ETS test. ETS has tried to get states using the same ETS test to agree on a common pass score, but so far it has not succeeded. NES states also determine their own pass scores. Only pass scores on the tests prepared by ABCTE provide comparable information across states; they are predetermined for each test and states may not alter them.

Fourth and far more problematic: No information is available for any state on any of its required tests on how many test items need to be correct (before the total number is converted to a scaled score) in order for a candidate to achieve a pass score.

Thus, for a number of reasons, the public has no way of knowing exactly what a pass score means academically on any teacher test in any state. In June 2002, in a caustic commentary on the first Title II report on the quality of teacher preparation in the 50 states put out by the U.S. Department of Education, Education Trust noted that most pass scores are set at or below the 25th percentile.[1] In other words, pass scores on most state tests are set so low that the vast majority of test takers pass.

WHAT WE KNOW ABOUT THE CONTENT OF TEACHER LICENSURE TESTS

We know from only one study, but a very good one, that a licensure test of teacher skills serves as an extremely minimal quality control for admission into a teacher preparation program, whether it is given at the undergraduate or graduate level. Ruth Mitchell and Patte Barth examined the content of a number of skills tests for their review of licensure tests in 1999.[2] With a team of academic experts to assist them, they judged ETS's PRAXIS I test to be at a middle school level in overall difficulty—before a pass score was set. Although they did not provide any details on the quality of the test items used to assess prospective teachers' reading skills, they judged two-thirds of the mathematics items on the PRAXIS I test to be at the middle school level, noting that it contained fewer items on algebra and geometry than on the 1996 grade 8 National Assessment of Educational Progress (NAEP) mathematics test. While praising the sample items on the skills test for prospective teachers and administrators in Massachusetts, a test they considered more complex and demanding than any of the other exams that they had reviewed, nevertheless, they maintained that none of the skills reviewed was at the level of a graduating college senior. At most, they argued, the various tests of teachers' reading, writing, and arithmetic skills were at the "8th to 10th (sometimes 7th) grade level" (p. 10).

After reviewing the content of some subject area tests as well, they reported that subject area tests, depending on the field, may not be much greater in difficulty than the skills tests they had reviewed. They judged the content tests required for elementary licensure as a whole at about the 10th grade level, before a pass score was set, even though prospective elementary teachers are required in all states to be college graduates.

POINTS TO REMEMBER

1. Only a few organizations—all private—provide teacher licensure tests in this country.

2. There are four types of licensure tests for prospective teachers, only one of which assesses their knowledge of the subjects they will teach.

3. Licensure tests of teacher's subject area knowledge may be given at different times in the professional education of a prospective teacher, unlike licensure tests for other professions, which can be taken only after completion of a professional training program.

4. The most comprehensive study of the content of teacher licensure tests, published in 1999, concluded that most are likely at the high school level in difficulty, despite the requirement that prospective teachers must have completed a four-year college degree program.

NOTES

1. Sandra Huang, Yun Yi, and Kati Haycock, *Interpret With Caution: The First State Title II Reports on the Quality of Teacher Preparation* (Washington, DC: The Education Trust, June 2002).

2. Ruth Mitchell and Patte Barth, "Not Good Enough: A Content Analysis of Teacher Licensing Examinations. How Teacher Licensing Tests Fall Short," *Thinking K–16*, 1999, 3(1), 3–23.

4

HISTORY OF TEACHER LICENSURE TESTS IN THE UNITED STATES

The history of teacher licensure tests officially begins in the late 1920s—when an emphasis on school efficiency and accountability was fueled by a thriving industry of achievement and intelligence testing. This emphasis took place in the context of a massive increase in the size and number of the nation's high schools to accommodate the children of those who had migrated to this country from the 1880s to World War I, as well as those children now forbidden factory employment or required to stay in school until age 16 because of Child Labor Laws passed in the early decades of the 20th century. The academic deficiencies of most teacher tests today can be traced to the self-interest of teacher educators in the 20th century—and the test makers they influenced.

EARLY TEACHER EXAMINATIONS

Examinations for teachers were first used in the United States in colonial New England.[1] Their origins were the examinations used to certify teachers at European, church-sponsored universities. In this country, potential teachers of a community's children needed to convince local ministers of their moral character, soundness of faith, as well as academic accomplishments. As public schooling expanded, especially after compulsory education was initiated in Massachusetts in 1852, teacher examinations spread throughout the country. They expanded to the state level once states entered the Union, although cities and counties often retained their own examinations, typically focused on a candidate's moral character and knowledge of common school subjects.

A considerable amount of content knowledge (and, correspondingly, very little pedagogical knowledge) was assessed on these examinations, as suggested by an investigation of the teacher tests given in 19th-century Wisconsin and California and turn-of-the-20th century Michigan by Richard Askey, a mathematician at the University of Wisconsin.[2] The credits for the 20 topics on the March 1875 exam in 19th-century California totaled 1000. The grade levels for which a license would be valid depended on getting a certain number of credits in key areas (Written Grammar and Spelling). Rote memorization was clearly not expected by most test questions. Askey gives the following examples of history questions for candidates who wanted to teach in grammar school in Michigan on an exam in 1900:

1. Tell what work was accomplished by Miltiades, and state its effect upon the country.
2. Briefly describe Ireland during the reign of Elizabeth.
3. Briefly state the result and effect of the Battle of Waterloo, naming the leading general.
4. (a) What was the bone of contention between Austria and Germany in 1866? (b) Give the result and effect of this trouble.
5. Name the leaders of the Italian struggle for freedom, and state the result of their efforts.
6. Mention some supplementary reading that you would recommend in a history class.
7. When was the present form of government in France organized, and who is president today?

Candidates did not have to be more than a high school graduate then. Today, it is unlikely that a college graduate aiming for a "middle school" license could satisfactorily answer similar essay questions.

Certification by examination was eventually supplanted by the acceptance of credentials showing completion of a prescribed sequence of school or college courses as college and normal school training programs expanded in the second half of the 19th century and the early decades of the 20th. Although mandatory examinations declined in the early 20th century, they continued in many large cities largely because of the demand for urban teaching positions. In rural areas, examinations were used to grant "emergency" licenses to candidates who had not completed professional training. Despite some criticism of the quality of these examinations, their use was considered unavoidable. Training institutions did not graduate enough candidates to fill the growing number of teaching positions available. An examination could assure a community of a minimal level of teacher competence, an assurance that graduation from a training institution apparently gave.

TEACHER TESTS IN THE 20TH CENTURY

A major impetus for the development of teacher tests was a 1920 Pennsylvania study of the relationships between the state's secondary and higher education systems. The study showed that prospective teachers had tested particularly poorly on the tests that had been developed to examine these relationships. Then as now, it appeared that those attracted to teaching varied widely in their academic ability and tended to "fall below a knowledge minimum in a large proportion of cases."

The development of teacher tests, especially for those seeking a high school position, was further stimulated by the Great Depression when school superintendents found a surplus of highly educated people available for teaching positions because of a lack of other jobs in their discipline-based specialties. The dilemma faced by superintendents was how to narrow down the pool to select the best teachers. From that dilemma, the American Council on Education gave birth to the National Teachers Examinations (NTE).

The first examinations, administered in 1940, assessed basic intellectual and communicative skills, cultural and contemporary background, and professional information. Only about 30 percent of a very long examination—well over eight hours—was on pedagogy and professional knowledge. Aspiring high school teachers also took a separate test on the content of the subject they hoped to teach. Test use was judged most successful in the urban areas of the New England and Middle Atlantic states where the practice of examining teaching candidates was already established and where a substantial surplus of teacher candidates existed.

From the very beginning, critics, many of whom were teacher educators, asked whether those who scored well on the NTE were also recognized later as good teachers—implying that this was the criterion for determining validity. That is, did the tests have predictive power? This question has bedeviled research on teacher tests from their onset. Test developers at the time argued that the validity of the tests could not be judged by correlating them with later "teaching success" because that was not the purpose of these tests and that what mattered was "construct validity" (i.e., to what extent the tests measured what they claimed to measure). Test developers further pointed out that "teaching success" could not be defined.

Nevertheless, education researchers correlated teacher test scores with supervisors' or principals' ratings. Their finding of only a moderate correlation was used by educators to raise doubts about the validity of these teacher tests, despite what test developers themselves had indicated was their purpose and nature, and to insist that validity could be determined only in relationship to student achievement after teachers began teaching.

GROWING INFLUENCE OF TEACHER EDUCATORS AFTER WORLD WAR II

After World War II, there was no longer a surplus of highly qualified people for teaching positions (indeed, there was a shortage), so the demand and funding for the NTE declined. Superintendents had no interest in test scores when the law required a teacher in every classroom. To address the lack of interest in the tests and to mollify teacher educators, testing time was reduced to three hours by 1951, the section on professional knowledge and pedagogy was weighted more (from 30 percent to 40 percent), the section on cultural knowledge and intellectual skills was weighted less, and the composition and leadership of the national advisory committee were changed to include more teacher educators.

Major changes were made in the mid-1960s in test purpose and validation by Educational Testing Service, now in charge of the NTE after taking over the project in the 1950s. Although only 39 percent was still weighted for professional knowledge and pedagogy, and the question of "what knowledge is of most worth to prospective teachers?" was to be considered in test development, the purpose of the test was now to provide "objective exams of measurable knowledges and abilities . . . commonly considered basic to effective classroom teaching and which typically constituted major elements in current programs of teacher education." Moreover, even though ETS's Technical Handbook, issued in 1965, stated that "the chief purpose of the NTE is to provide an independent evaluation of the academic preparation of teacher education students," the validating criterion for the content of the test was now how the test related to teacher education curricula. Since the academic preparation of most prospective teachers occurred in the arts and sciences, not in education schools, this criterion made no sense. Worse yet, it excluded the very sources of validation that would have made sense—the syllabi developed by academic experts for their courses in the arts and sciences.

The 1970s introduced new issues that ultimately had a major effect on the academic quality of the NTE. A series of court challenges had contended that the NTE had a racially discriminatory effect on minority employment in the public schools. The defining moment occurred in 1978 when the U.S. Supreme Court refused to accept a case against use of the NTE in South Carolina for teacher certification and affirmed the 1977 decision of a Federal District Court, which had stated, "The State has the right to adopt academic requirements and to use written tests designed and validated to disclose the minimum amount of knowledge necessary to effective teaching." Although states were judged to have the right to set academic requirements for prospective teachers, the decision implicitly affirmed a methodology for determining content validity that would, in the long-term, undermine the basic purpose for teacher licensure tests.

To determine the content validity of the NTE, ETS had earlier used some 450 faculty members from about 25 teacher training institutions in South Carolina to judge whether or not the content of each question was covered *by the teacher education program.* Thus, teacher educators' judgments on the minimum amount of academic knowledge needed to complete a teacher education program came to serve as the basis for the passing scores for all NTE tests—a model from whose chilling grip teacher licensure tests have yet to be fully emancipated. On what rational basis could researchers determine whether the "estimates of the percentages of minimally knowledgeable candidates who would be expected to know the answers to individual test questions" were related to effective teaching when the "knowledge estimation panels" providing these estimates were dominated by judges who were hostile to content knowledge? Their basic concern was protecting the right of anyone to teach, regardless of academic competence, not the right of children to be taught by academically knowledgeable teachers.

RISING DEMAND FOR TEACHER LICENSURE TESTS IN THE 1970S AND 1980S

A growing demand for teacher testing in the late 1970s and early 1980s led ETS to set up an external board (Policy Council) to govern and direct NTE program policies. By 1982, the Policy Council, which now included classroom teachers as well as teacher educators, guided another revision of the NTE, validated by teacher educators and classroom teachers against the curricula in teacher training schools. The Council reiterated that the basic purpose of the tests was "to provide a measure of academic preparation for beginning teachers," but, clearly, its understanding of "academic preparation" referred to what was taught in education schools, not the academic coursework that should underlie the subjects they would teach. It was in fact ironic that the tests were validated on the basis of their similarity to the curricula of teacher training institutions even though teacher testing was from its inception promoted on the grounds that teacher training institutions were graduating academically inadequate teachers. In any event, the tests were not taken seriously as a measure of teachers' academic knowledge and skills, and critics, including the teacher unions but especially Albert Shanker, president of the American Federation of Teachers, urged ETS to develop stronger tests.

As public concern about the quality of the teachers graduating from our education schools continued to mount, ETS developed its PRAXIS series in the late 1980s on the ashes of the NTE but with the dominant influence of the education schools intact. The testing of prospective and practicing teachers increased enormously in the 1980s, mainly as a result of the wave of school-improvement efforts enacted around the country. In 1977, only Mississippi and North Carolina required new teachers to pass statewide licensing examinations. By 1988, 43 states did, but ETS's tests were no longer the only game in town. A second company (NES) was now developing teacher licensure tests.

CONGRESSIONAL REQUIREMENT IN 1998 OF LICENSURE TESTS FOR ALL PROSPECTIVE TEACHERS

In the fall of 1998, Congress passed legislation requiring teacher tests in every state. This legislation was a direct consequence of the results of the first administration of Massachusetts's own teacher tests in the spring of 1998. In 1993, a far-reaching Massachusetts Education Reform Act (MERA) had specified a measure of accountability for each major component of public education. For education schools, the measure was teacher testing—at least two different tests, one of teachers' reading and writing skills and the other of teachers' knowledge of the subject matter of their license. National Evaluation Systems developed the Bay State's first teacher tests using the teacher preparation program regulations in place at the time as their legal basis. The first administration of over 40 subject matter tests took place in the spring of 1998.

Although education schools (which had unsuccessfully opposed the requirement in MERA) were under the impression that these were only pilot tests for prospective teachers and didn't want the dismal results publicized, a close to 60 percent failure rate attracted national headlines. Both the U.S. Department of Education and Congress were so appalled by this failure rate that they quickly inserted into Title II of the 1998 reauthorization of the Higher Education Act the requirement that each state test each cohort of prospective teachers and report their individual preparation programs' pass rates annually to the U.S. Department of Education. That provision compelled all states to require licensure tests for new teachers.

Each state henceforth had to report annually on the pass rates on tests of its own choosing for each cohort of prospective teachers completing training programs in the state's own teacher training institutions. However, each state was allowed to decide what licensure tests it would require, what it would assess on them, their pass scores, and when the tests could be taken. The expectation was that a requirement to report pass scores on state licensure tests annually would upgrade the quality of the teacher preparation programs in each state or perhaps cause some to go out of existence. And, within a few years, almost all institutions in all states were reporting almost 100 percent pass rates. But this was not because of higher admission standards and/or academically stronger programs (or because weak programs went out of existence). None of this took place, as suggested by a 2002 Education Trust report on the effects of this Title II provision and by several studies on the content of preparation programs for elementary teachers, to be discussed in a later chapter.

POINTS TO REMEMBER

1. Prospective teachers in most states in the 19th and early 20th centuries were expected to pass short but demanding tests of their academic knowledge and/or to provide a transcript of their course of studies in college or a teacher training school.

2. The first nationwide tests, the National Teachers Examinations, were offered in 1940. They were developed to help many large cities and states to determine the best candidates in a large pool of academically qualified candidates seeking a teaching career during the Great Depression.

3. Almost from the beginning, teacher educators claimed that subject matter tests could be validated only by evidence of teachers' later effectiveness, even though the test developers insisted that the validity of subject matter tests depended only on whether they could be shown to measure what they claimed to measure—the test taker's academic knowledge. They pointed out that there was no agreement on what teacher effectiveness meant, never mind how to measure it.

4. Tests of academic knowledge needed to show construct validity. But teacher educators then, as now, were not interested in assessing either the teachers' or the students' content knowledge.

5. In 1998, a reauthorization of the Higher Education Act required all states to submit test scores annually for each cohort of prospective teachers completing their teacher preparation programs,

in effect requiring all states to develop or provide licensure tests. But the federal government did not specify what should be on the tests, where the cut score should be, or when the tests should be given.

NOTES

1. Ann Jarvella Wilson, "Knowledge for Teachers: The Origin of the National Teacher Examinations Program," paper presented at the Annual Meeting of the American Educational Research Association, Chicago, Illinois, April 1985, ED 262 049. All material on early teacher examinations is taken from Wilson's paper, which is based on her dissertation, "Knowledge for Teachers: The National Teacher Examinations Program, 1940–1970," University of Wisconsin, 1984, University Microfilms International No. 84-14265.

2. Richard Askey, "Examinations for Teachers in the Past and Present," Schoolinfosystem.org. http://www.schoolinfosystem.org/pdf/2007/04/askeymadlit.pdf.

5

WHAT GENERATES TOPICS ON SUBJECT AREA LICENSING TESTS?

What should a state test aspiring teachers on before giving them a license to teach the subject(s) or children they want to teach? How much can parents reasonably expect teachers to know about the subject(s) they hope to teach their children? Common sense suggests that test makers should be guided by the depth and breadth of the content taught at the grade levels teachers want to teach. Common sense also suggests that teachers should know much more about the subject they want to teach than they are apt to have to teach to even the quickest learners in their classrooms. However, common sense has played a limited role in the construction of these tests and especially in the setting of a pass score.

At their inception, teacher licensure tests were intended to ensure a high level of academic competence in a prospective teacher, not minimal competence. The examination questions used in 19th- and early 20th-century Wisconsin and California make that clear. They were not intended to keep out just the grossly academically incompetent would-be teacher who should have been weeded out long before taking a licensure test. They were not intended to reward with a license those with barely a minimal command of the subjects they hoped to teach—the seeming purpose of most teacher subject licensure tests today.

The academic experts who reviewed the content of a number of teacher licensure tests for Mitchell and Barth's 1999 study raised a different issue. These experts wondered why a college degree is required of a prospective teacher after examining tests ranging in academic demand, in their judgment, from middle school level to upper high school level.[1] What they did not go on to explore is how academically impoverished teacher licensure tests might shape the school curriculum, especially in areas where no statewide test for students casts a challenging shadow on what teachers teach. Nor did they look at what generates the content of licensing tests.

HOW THE CONTENT OF TEACHER LICENSING TESTS MAY BE DESIGNATED

Educator licensing regulations typically contain many sections, each addressing an important matter such as criteria for approving educator preparation programs (also known as "program approval"), professional standards for teachers and administrators, and requirements for initial and full licensure. Such a document must guide teacher preparation programs with respect to the *academic* coursework their students should take (or should have taken before admission) to become teachers of a particular subject (e.g., history) or type of student (e.g., special needs). Such a document must also guide the selection or development of licensure tests of aspiring teachers' academic knowledge in all the fields for which licenses are given.

The section on academic requirements for the different fields in which licenses are given has several very different audiences: arts and sciences faculty, who learn from this section as well as from education school colleagues what courses they need to provide aspiring teachers of their subject; an accreditation team trying to determine if the graduates of an education school's preparation programs are adequately prepared for the license they seek and the classes they would teach; and the test developer. The most important audience for this section of the regulations is the audience *least* likely to read a document on licensing regulations: arts and sciences faculty in the state's institutions of higher education.

RELIANCE ON A COLLEGE MAJOR OR MINOR

Academic requirements for each field are indicated in different ways in licensing regulations. In an extreme hands-off approach, many states' regulations simply require prospective teachers (typically secondary teachers) to major in the discipline if they want to teach a secondary subject, or to complete a "teaching major" (often a less academically rigorous form of the major). This easy way out in licensing regulations for secondary teachers has a major downside. It means the test developer has to search out descriptions of coursework required for a major in the state's colleges and pull together the chief topics in them. (Needless to say, if the state is planning to use an off-the-shelf licensure test from the ETS PRAXIS series, then no test developer is involved.)

For prospective generalists (e.g., elementary and special education teachers), the regulations may indicate very broadly the subject areas or professional topics they need to have studied. But in states where they are expected to major in an academic discipline, that discipline may turn out to be an undergraduate program in child development as a special program in the psychology department.

In a less extreme hands-off approach, regulations offer a few broad statements of what aspiring teachers should study (often to guide a licensure test developer). This was the approach in the 1994 Massachusetts regulations. For example, they required teachers of a foreign language to major in the language and demonstrate knowledge of "the varieties of the language(s) and the associated cultures, histories and literature, including those of native language speakers in the U.S." With vaster aspirations, they required teachers of English to major in English and demonstrate knowledge of "history and studies of language; English, American and world literature; theories of language acquisition; written and oral composition; drama; and speech communication."[2]

Such broad statements give enormous leeway to the test developer in generating test objectives. In addition, colleges in even one state often differ in the content of the coursework they require for a major or a minor in a particular discipline, so a testing company must use its judgment about what objectives to test and how to weight them.

USEFULNESS OF A TOPIC APPROACH

Not surprisingly, some faculty in Massachusetts colleges complained that the 1994 regulations gave too much leeway to the test developer. After examining the regulations in other states—and discussing with college faculty in the Bay State the problems they perceived in the licensure tests first given in 1998—my staff and I decided to work out a short list of key academic topics for each field that would function as major objectives for the licensure test for that field. Such lists would tell arts and sciences faculty what their courses needed to cover and what a subject area licensure test needed to assess. For the sake of equity alone, we agreed that all teachers should take coursework in topics that inform what they are expected to teach (e.g., for history teachers, the philosophical antecedents of the U.S. Constitution), whether or not a college course on the topic is required for a major in the discipline.

A topic approach is a powerful way to strengthen a prospective teacher's academic background regardless of the college he or she attends as an undergraduate. It differs from what is done in many states' regulations with respect to specificity. It lists the major academic topics for each field—not as many as would be listed on individual syllabi, but enough to clarify the intellectual highlights of a field. The link in the following endnote leads to the topics listed for each field in the Bay State's licensing regulations.[3]

These lists for each licensing test identify, to the extent possible, those topics that candidates for a particular teaching license should study in their arts and sciences major and in other arts and sciences courses. They reflect as comprehensively as possible the relevant academic background for the K–12 content standards the prospective teacher will be expected to teach to, and at the educational level for which the candidate seeks licensure. To be approved for reaccreditation, teacher training programs must demonstrate how students in their programs can cover these topics in arts and sciences coursework. The list of topics for each subject area license excludes, to the extent possible, professional or pedagogical skills and knowledge.

For simplicity's sake, why not simply require a particular major, a choice from a restricted set of majors, or a specific number of credit hours in a discipline, to ensure that a prospective teacher of X is academically prepared to teach the relevant subject matter? These often-used methods in many states' licensing regulations are academic short-cuts that no longer work, for three reasons. First, they no longer necessarily signify that the person completing a major or the required credit hours in, for example, the humanities has addressed the academic content that is relevant to teaching K–12 students. Second, both training programs and interested candidates need to know what specific coursework is deemed useful for precollege teaching; they need some guidance in constructing their course of study. Third, licensure tests for teachers need external validity. When an agency of the state determines the academic content needed for a teaching license, it provides the legal basis for the content of the licensing test and program.

A topic approach does not require much if any involvement of education faculty since what is being determined is academic content. Unknown to most arts and sciences faculty, regulations for prospective K–12 teachers reach deep into the arts and sciences precisely because they must indicate the academic requirements for each licensure field. While regulations cannot usurp the prerogatives of an academic faculty in determining the content of a major, they can serve to strengthen the academic background a prospective teacher acquires by virtue of their specificity.

HOW SUBJECT AREA LICENSURE TESTS FOR TEACHERS INDIRECTLY SHAPE THE SCHOOL CURRICULUM

Licensure tests for early childhood, elementary, and special education teachers have had an immense influence on the entire school curriculum because most have been shaped almost monolithically by one side in the "reading" wars. New elementary teachers tend to shape their reading programs as they were taught in their reading methods coursework and then assessed for licensure. As a result, many have learned to disdain the teaching strategies associated with "learning the code" (e.g., teacher-directed instruction), often on the grounds that such instruction has alienated children from learning to read, even though a large, credible body of research-based evidence supports teacher-directed instruction and the strategies associated with it. As I found in my own research, many may also learn from test items on licensure tests to discredit teacher-directed instruction, i.e., what is supported by credible research."[4]

Licensure tests for these three groups of teachers have in some cases simply ignored the teaching of beginning reading (e.g., most tests designed for special education teachers). In other cases, they have assessed beginning reading instructional knowledge so minimally that text takers' lack of knowledge in this crucial area hasn't affected the overall results; compensatory scoring has disguised text takers' failures on critical sections of these tests (i.e., reading and mathematics).

How do licensure tests of beginning reading instructional knowledge that promote the context-based methods taught in most education schools influence the school curriculum and long-term student achievement? If students are taught to use context or a word's visual pattern to guess at the identification of a word already in their listening vocabulary, and to use context to guess at the meaning of a word that needs to enter their reading vocabulary, that habit slows down the speed at which they can read more advanced texts throughout the grades, reducing the amount they can read altogether. And if they are not taught to "sound out" more difficult multi-syllabic words by syllables (words often within their listening vocabulary), they will be less accurate readers with academic materials as they progress through school. Silent reading practice and peer-led group discussions (i.e., no oral reading groups led by the teacher) serve to disguise lack of speed as well as a student's difficulty in pronouncing multi-syllabic words accurately and then recognizing their meaning.

Perhaps the most serious damage has been inflicted on those students who need to rely on the schools to help them acquire an ever-increasing and increasingly important technical vocabulary in mathematics, history, geography, and the sciences. These are the students who do not have highly literate parents to compensate for a mistrained teacher's insistence that they rely on context and daily life to learn the technical language of these other subjects, rather than use a glossary or footnotes. As mathematicians and scientists are quick to point out, many common technical terms have specific meanings that differ from the meanings attached to them in daily life (e.g., table, rate, force). In addition, the first meanings in a dictionary for such words are apt to be their most common meanings, not the technical meaning.

There are also negative consequences for K–12 from the kind of licensure tests prospective foreign language teachers are now apt to take—tests that focus on the daily language skills for the target language and slight the literate cultures of the countries using that language, especially the literate culture of the country of origin of the target language. A licensure test that deliberately minimizes (by its weight) the intellectual, historical, and artistic culture of the country of origin of the target language, often to spite its historical role as a colonizing empire, is apt to lead foreign language teachers to create and/or implement an academically impoverished curriculum for their students, leaving American students with little understanding of the broader culture in which the target language is situated.

It is apparently politically incorrect to assess on a licensure test a prospective foreign language teacher's knowledge of the intellectual and artistic culture of the language's country of origin, especially if it is Spain. It may also be politically incorrect to teach about Spain's intellectual and artistic culture in K–12, as well. Although no research on the cultural content of the elementary and secondary school Spanish curriculum in this country can be found, American students may be learning little about the development of the language and the literary, artistic, and intellectual history of its country of origin when they study any European language in K–12. The relatively small number of college students majoring in a foreign language aside from Spanish in this country may thus be a reflection of the limitations of their K–12 foreign language curriculum.

The richness of the school curriculum is clearly affected by licensure tests for teachers of communication and the performing arts that deliberately ignore cultural specifics. Most are "low-incidence" tests because they are taken by relatively few test takers. But even if there is only one art, music, dance, speech, or drama teacher for an elementary or middle school, that one teacher is apt to reach all the students in that school, unlike the teacher in one self-contained elementary classroom. The school may schedule a music, art, or dance class only once or twice a week, but these classes, together with schoolwide opportunities for performance, enable a teacher of a performing art to broaden all students' aesthetic and cultural horizons (and excite their interest) in ways that major subject area teachers need far more time to do.

It is not clear that today's art or dance teachers provide their young students with the broad cultural education that music teachers may still do, to judge by the content of their licensure tests in the Bay State. This is a loss to the prospective teacher's own education but even more so to hundreds of thousands of K–12 students. They can no longer be stimulated by remnants of an abandoned liberal education that teachers of earlier generations could impart, knowing that familiarity with significant figures, movements, and works in the evolution of their art form was often the wellspring of their students' creativity. For example, as noted in the next chapter, while music school faculty in Bay State licensure programs seek to broaden prospective teachers' understanding of contemporary music and musical traditions around the globe, they also ensure that a prospective music teacher has some familiarity with the history of our dynamic Western musical tradition, from ancient Greece and church music in the Middle Ages through major European composers—as well as an understanding of the theoretical concepts underlying this tradition.

It is still not clear how prepared any English teacher today is to teach what students in American public schools should study in grades 6–12. The weights in a test profile may look right, but the pass score may undo academic demands. For example, in Massachusetts, 51 percent of the test addresses literature and language. But the pass rate is between 80–90 percent annually, suggesting that the pass score is not high enough. A relatively low pass score (leading to a high pass rate) could mean that questions drawing on presumed coursework in classic texts from American or British literature may not be answered correctly but, because of compensatory scoring, won't matter for the final score.

Nevertheless, the specificity of the topics in licensing regulations can make a difference in the college curriculum. A professor of English at a state university in Massachusetts casually commented at a conference for literary scholars in April 2014 that the demands of the topics on the licensure test for prospective English teachers in the Bay State had led to a stronger set of course requirements for these undergraduates than for the English major itself at her university.

Perhaps the most damaged subjects in the school curriculum today are history and government, but not necessarily because of teacher training programs or licensing tests. If teacher licensing tests reflect the content and spirit of what prospective teachers are now taught in their majors (or minors) in these disciplines (and/or in other courses at the undergraduate level), then K–12 students may well be deprived by their teachers of what they need to understand most from them—the basic political principles, procedures, and processes on which our particular democracy rests at all levels of government. If their teachers do not attempt to supplement what may be in current instructional materials, young students will fail to learn how these political principles evolved historically, where they failed to advance freedom and justice and why, where they succeeded in advancing freedom and justice and why, and why these political principles are worth preserving in today's world.

The current nationwide controversy over the revised contents of the Advanced Placement U.S. History syllabus and test is but one example of where these problems may play out. We do not hear much, if anything, from the high school teachers of this revised course about how they will address its ideological bent, if at all. The topics for the new licensing tests for teachers of history or U.S. government in the Bay State ensure that significant texts (such as the *Federalist Papers*) will be assessed and, by implication, required in coursework for "program approval."

NOTES

1. Ruth Mitchell and Patte Barth, "Not Good Enough: A Content Analysis of Teacher Licensing Examinations. How Teacher Licensing Tests Fall Short," *Thinking K–16*, 1999, 3(1), 3–23.

2. Massachusetts Department of Education, Regulations for the Certification of Educational Personnel in Massachusetts, April 1995, p. 68.

3. 603 CMR 7.00: Regulations for Educator Licensure and Preparation Program Approval, Massachusetts Department of Elementary and Secondary Education. http://www.doe.mass.edu/lawsregs/603cmr7.html?section=06.

4. Sandra Stotsky, "Licensure Tests for Special Education Teachers: How Well They Assess Knowledge of Reading Instruction and Mathematics," *Journal of Learning Disabilities*, September/October 2009, 42(5), 464–74. http://ldx.sagepub.com/cgi/content/abstract/42/5/464.

6

RATIONALE FOR NEW AND OLD LICENSES IN THE BAY STATE

The Massachusetts Education Reform Act (MERA) of 1993 sought to strengthen the academic background of new teachers by mandating teacher tests of subject area knowledge. I was able to draw on the objectives I had formulated to guide the revision of the state's K–12 standards for the revision of the state's licensure tests, as all were being revised at the same time. Spelled out in more detail in an essay published in 2004 by the Brookings Institution, my main objectives for upgrading the K–12 standards in each subject were, briefly:

1. To restore disciplinary learning to the central place in each subject area,
2. To make the organization of the content of high school standards compatible with the normal disciplinary training of current and prospective teachers of that subject,
3. To make explicit and coherent the content to be taught by teachers in each subject area,
4. To lay the academic groundwork in middle and early high school for advanced coursework in grades 11 and 12,
5. To provide school districts with options for curricular sequences wherever possible. [1]

It quickly became apparent that, in order to address MERA's goal of attracting to a teaching career a larger number of academically able arts and sciences majors, we would have to create new licenses as well as revise old ones, especially for the upper elementary and middle school. To do so, we would have to specify the topics that would be assessed on the licensure tests for these new licenses. This would, in turn, stimulate development of licensure programs leading to them.

One group of new licenses was designed for full-time teachers of mathematics, science, foreign languages, and history/geography in the elementary grades. These are simply subject area licenses for the elementary level rather than, as is traditional, for the secondary level. Hiring people with these licenses would allow elementary schools to organize the middle to upper elementary grades with subject-divided days, with each major subject taught by a knowledgeable teacher of that subject, rather than as self-contained classrooms taught by a generalist elementary teacher with weak academic knowledge in most, if not all, of the many subjects she typically teaches.

A second group of licenses was designed to address the academic weaknesses of current middle school teachers—the educational level where it is most urgent to upgrade our teaching force. We created: (1) a combined English and history license and a combined mathematics and science license, each requiring at least 36 credit hours of coursework; (2) a separate middle school mathematics license; and (3) a separate middle school general science license. We also developed tests of the content for each license. The goal was to make them less demanding than tests for aspiring high school teachers of these subjects, but more demanding than tests of that content for prospective elementary teachers.

A third group of new licenses was designed to remedy currently weak academic preparation in three different but increasingly important areas. One license was for teaching students in the public schools whose first language is not English after the state's voters passed an initiative petition to end "transitional bilingual education," a poorly thought-through approach to teaching English to non-English-speaking students. The license for the teacher of English language learners highlighted English immersion and the "sheltered" teaching of academic content as well as of English language and literacy skills. This one license eventually eliminated "transitional bilingual education" licenses for teachers of ten different languages.

The second license was for political science/political philosophy. The license (and its title) was designed to attract undergraduate or graduate students in philosophy or political science to high school teaching of U.S. or comparative government.

The third license in this group was a specialist license designed for teaching academically advanced students in K–8 in order to address a population of students slighted by the attention to disabled learners. The license required an academically strong teacher whose main task was to find ways to provide accelerated learning for high academic achievers in K–8.

All are described below in more detail, along with existing licenses we were revising, in the broad subject area in which they are often classified by licensing test developers, by type, or by educational level. I indicate how we tried to strengthen the academic requirements for people seeking an initial teaching license in the area and the issues we faced.

LICENSURE TESTS FOR FOREIGN LANGUAGE TEACHERS

My goal in 1999 was to clarify the academic goals and requirements of a license for teachers of a language other than English from the elementary through the secondary grades. My interest in this area stemmed from my undergraduate major in French literature and language and my experience teaching French and German in high school. What academic knowledge and skills should one expect foreign language teachers to bring to their first classrooms? Little did I expect this question to lead to a minefield called "cultural literacy," a phrase that I soon came to realize actually meant "cultural illiteracy."

Licensure Tests for Secondary Teachers of a Foreign Language

Spanish is the most frequently taught foreign language in Massachusetts public schools as well as in the country at large, followed at a considerably lower frequency by French. My first step was to seek advice from college faculty who taught foreign languages and supervised student teachers in K–12. What did they think was the appropriate academic coursework to assess on a licensure test for someone planning to teach in the public schools, *not coursework for a major or minor*? What problems had they found in the original foreign language tests or in the 1994 regulations? Ironically, the major problem was the requirement for multicultural literacy and the influence of an unrelenting egalitarian multiculturalism on the test items. Under the 1994 regulations, test takers for a license to teach French or Spanish had to prepare themselves to answer questions addressing the following three broad objectives under a category labeled "Cultural Understanding":

1. Understand major developments in the history of cultures associated with the target language and the cultural significance of those developments.
2. Understand geographic, economic, social, and political features of contemporary cultures associated with the target language, including the ways in which values influence these features.
3. Understand literature, the nonliterary arts, science, and technology as aspects of cultures associated with the target language.

Even if a college's foreign language department deliberately avoided the high culture of the country of origin of a particular language (on the ideological ground that it had been the center of an oppressive empire), it was not possible for the department to provide prospective K–12 teachers with sufficient coursework on *every single country using the target language* so that they would be prepared for randomly generated test questions on any one of them.

The failure rates on the Spanish and French tests were, in the judgment of Spanish and French language college faculty, a reflection of the vast range of Spanish-speaking and French-speaking countries about which questions were asked. Over a four-year period (from 1998–2001), only 69 percent (203 of 294) of those taking the French test had passed it, while only 79 percent (660 of 833) had passed the Spanish test—to Spanish and French college faculty an unacceptably low percentage. These college faculty members wanted standards that limited a test taker's knowledge to just the "mother" country and one other country using the target language. So, based on their advice, the seven broad, generic topics listed below were developed as objectives for a licensure test for grades 5–12. These still appear in the licensing regulations, although they do not govern current licensure tests in foreign languages in the Bay State. I will explain why later.

1. Spoken and written command of a standard version of the target language (the version used by a formally educated speaker of the language).
2. Knowledge of culturally and historically significant literary and nonliterary texts and authors associated with the country of origin of the target language; literary traditions, periods, and genres.
3. Introductory knowledge of the other arts (historical traditions, genres, and major artists) associated with the country of origin of the target language.
4. Introductory knowledge of the political, social, and intellectual history of the country or culture with which the target language is or was originally associated.
5. Introductory knowledge of significant literary and nonliterary texts, the arts, and history of at least one other country or people with which the target language may now be associated.
6. Similarities and differences between the target language and English.
7. Theories of, and differences between, first- and second-language acquisition.

This short list was reasonable; #5 reduced to "one other" the many countries now using the target language whose people, history, customs, literature, and government college students had been implicitly compelled to become familiar with in order to pass the existing tests. Only college faculty knew what a difference that one objective would make—and what a relief it would be to them.

At the time I left the department in September 2003, drafts of strands and weights for the template of a revised foreign language test had begun circulating, and a few advisory meetings had taken place devoted to Spanish. They were attended mainly by Spanish language teachers and specialists in the schools who, it turned out, were not aware of the complaints about the existing Spanish test by college faculty (so they claimed). These school people did not want a new test to stress cultural knowledge—literary, historical, intellectual (#2, #3, and #4)—or to confine cultural knowledge to the country of origin of the target language (Spain) and to only one other Spanish-speaking country (#5). They wanted the test to focus on language skills, grammar, and linguistic knowledge. I was at first dazed. Education schools and professional development programs constantly talk about the need for teachers to be "culturally competent." But not teachers of a foreign language, it seemed.

These school people, I soon came to understand, viewed the licensure test as a way to enforce what they wanted taught in the K–12 curriculum, not as an assessment of a future teacher's academic background for teaching a foreign language. In fact, they didn't want much cultural knowledge of any Spanish-speaking country assessed. If cultural knowledge had to be assessed, they didn't want it weighted more than 10 percent, an effective (if novel) way of solving the egalitarian multicultural dilemma. So far as I could tell, the implication was that K–12 students were not expected to learn much, if anything, about the history and literate culture of any Spanish-speaking country, especially the country of origin of the language itself (since it was the home of the oppressive Spanish empire).

The final profile of strands and weights that emerged by 2009 after a six-year battle simply ignored what was in the 2001 regulations. Below is the current template for the strands and weights for the grades 5–12 licensure test in Massachusetts for French, German, Spanish, Chinese, Italian, Russian, and Portuguese:

Multiple-Choice (70 items)	*Approximate Test Weighting*
I. Listening Comprehension	18%
II. Reading Comprehension	19%
III. Linguistics and Language Structures	18%
IV. Cultural Perspectives, Comparisons, and Connections	15%
Open-Response	
V. Written Expression	15%
VI. Oral Expression	15%

As can be seen, skills (listening comprehension, reading comprehension, written expression, and oral expression) total 67 percent of the weight of the test (18 percent, 19 percent, 15 percent, and 15 percent respectively). Grammatical knowledge is worth another 18 percent. The one section (Cultural Perspectives) that could help to determine whether the test taker has more than an elementary or middle school education in the target language is worth no more than 15 percent.

However, the Reading Comprehension section, I discovered, was used by some professors of French to signal that a higher level of cultural literacy is expected of the prospective high school teacher of French. Probably as a result of their advice, this section on the secondary French practice test (which had been developed to address complaints about the unacceptable-to-them pass rate on the secondary licensure test) features passages by such well-known writers in French literary history as Hugo, Balzac, and Flaubert.

In contrast, there are no test items on the secondary Spanish practice test that address what a college student has *likely* read as a major in Spanish literature (e.g., works by Cervantes or García Lorca) or what a high school student *may* read in an Advanced Placement course on Latin American literature. Indeed, unless the coursework required of a college Spanish major is far more academically demanding than the content of the secondary Spanish licensure test, the licensed teacher is unlikely to be able to teach an Advanced Placement course on Latin American literature, never mind the literature of Spain itself.

The disdain for the cultural knowledge that an educated speaker of a foreign language could draw on, as expressed in the 15 percent weight (about 15 questions) for that strand in the Massachusetts licensure tests for secondary teachers of a foreign language, is also evident in the licensure tests offered by Educational Testing Service. The PRAXIS II French Content Knowledge test (0173) offers 23 questions on Cultural Perspectives, worth 19 percent of the test, "designed to measure your knowledge of the cultures of France and Francophone countries and regions." The one sample question offered for that section is about the time for dinner in France, no doubt an important piece of cultural knowledge for a foreigner to learn. The PRAXIS II World Language test (5174) for French offers 15 questions on Cultural Knowledge, worth 12 percent of the test. One sample question is an excerpt from *Le Petit Chose* by Alphonse Daudet. Another is based on an interview with the president of the Ivorian National Assembly. Neither is a strong signal that a high level of cultural literacy will be assessed—or expected.

In a similar spirit, the sample question for Cultural Perspectives on the German Content Knowledge test is about Lichtenstein, while the sample question for the Culture section on the World Language test for German is about making sauerkraut. Nothing on Beethoven, Goethe, Heine, Schubert, or other world-famous cultural giants.

The Cultural Perspectives section on the Spanish Content Knowledge test (0191) purports to focus on "history, contemporary issues, geography, literature and the arts, lifestyles and societies of the Spanish-speaking world, and sociolinguistic elements of Spanish." Sample questions are on Mexico and the Incas. Sample questions on the World Language test for Spanish are on Mexico, Argentina, and the Arabic influence on the Spanish language. One begins to suspect that questions about the literary, musical, or artistic culture of the country of origin of the target language are forbidden. Yet, this is the cultural knowledge that is likely taught to high school students in all countries using the target language as a national language. This is akin to cutting off one's nose to spite one's face.

To judge by what is on licensure tests for prospective teachers of a foreign language in K–12 by ETS or for Spanish in Massachusetts, most educators on the Content Advisory Committees to the testing company have had little regard for the literate culture informing the language used by educated speakers of that language—cultural knowledge that the countries using the target language would expect of their own high school graduates, never mind of those who teach it. (It is unlikely that the Spanish tests developed by NES for other client states are different.) Other than Spain or Portugal itself, most countries using the Spanish or Portuguese language, for example, are apparently forever stamped as former colonies of an evil empire, thus justifying questions about them only because they are former colonies. One might think that since the language their inhabitants speak was informed by the literature and other artistic and intellectual achievements of the language's country of origin, questions about the artistic or intellectual culture of the country of origin would also be justified. But that does not seem to be the case.

Licensure Tests for Elementary Teachers of a Foreign Language

Not only is literate cultural knowledge of the country of origin for a target language seemingly unwanted in a prospective foreign language teacher for the secondary grades, so too, it seems, is the kind of cultural knowledge one would want in a foreign language teacher of young children. This is more than cutting off one's nose to spite one's face. The lack of appropriate training programs for elementary teachers of a foreign language smacks of masking the whole face to prevent anyone from seeing the damage.

Since teachers of young children in schools where English is the language of instruction are expected to know how to teach beginning reading and writing in English (as well as mathematics, science, history, and geography), why wouldn't the elementary teacher of Spanish, for example, know how beginning reading and writing is taught in Spanish and be familiar with high-quality children's literature written in Spanish?

So, with the help of college foreign language faculty, we developed two modest objectives on cultural knowledge of the country of origin of the target language and two new objectives that seemed eminently reasonable for a test for those teaching in the elementary school (#3 and #4 below). We discovered that such a test had never existed despite the large number of foreign language teachers licensed to teach young children. According to certification office records, from 1997 to 2001, several hundred test takers in Massachusetts had been issued elementary and middle school level licenses spanning a bewildering variety of grade levels (K–9, 5–9, 1–6, or K–3) for teaching a variety of foreign languages (mainly Spanish, though).

Test objectives were to address:

1. Knowledge of culturally and historically significant literary and nonliterary texts and authors associated with the country of origin of the target language and of one other country with which the target language may now be associated.
2. Introductory knowledge of contemporary political, social, and artistic features of the country of origin of the target language and of one other country with which the target language may now be associated.

3. Children's literature, songs, and games in the target language.
4. Characteristics of elementary reading and writing pedagogy in the target language.

As can be seen, what we expected was similar to what would be expected of an elementary teacher in any language, including English. Nor did we receive criticism on these two topics at the time. Yet, there is so far, in the Bay State, no licensure test for that level based on current regulations. The regulations simply indicate that the test for grades 5–12 is acceptable for K–6, even though there is nothing on that test to assure parents that the teachers hired to teach in an elementary bilingual or foreign language program know any literature, songs, or games written for children in the target language (# 3) or the pedagogy used for children in countries using the target language (# 4). PRAXIS II does not even bother to offer a licensure test for foreign language teachers at the elementary level.

One reason that American children do so poorly in learning other languages in K–12 (or learn so little) is clear. Foreign language teachers in this country are not trained to teach a foreign language in elementary schools in the same way the native language is taught here or in a country using that language. It is not at all clear why foreign language teachers in an elementary program, especially a bilingual program, should not be expected to be familiar with the stories, games, and songs that young children could easily learn in a foreign language.

Licensure Tests for Latin and Classical Humanities Teachers

Moving from the culturally impoverished background apparently desired for prospective elementary or secondary Spanish teachers, to judge by their licensure tests, to what is expected of secondary Latin teachers is like moving to another planet. Below are the topics developed in Massachusetts by a group of professors of the classics and still in the Bay State's teacher licensure regulations. These professors clearly intend to prepare culturally literate secondary teachers.

1. Selections commonly read in secondary schools from the works of Cicero, Caesar, Catullus, Vergil, Horace, Ovid, and Pliny the Younger in the original Latin.

2. How English words are derived and formed from Greek and Latin prefixes, bases, and suffixes, and the influence of Greek and Latin on the technical vocabulary of the arts, sciences, and professions (medical and legal).

3. Works of Greek literature in translation including Herodotus, Homer, Plato, Sappho, Thucydides, and the four major dramatists.

4. Culture and history of ancient Greece and Rome, with emphasis on those elements that contributed to the foundation of modern Western civilization, including:

   a. Major myths and legends,
   b. Significant characteristics of classical art, architecture, and technology,
   c. Major genres of literature,
   d. Political, social, and economic institutions.

5. Linguistics and theories of classical language acquisition.

6. Methods of research and criticism as they apply to the study of Latin and classical humanities.

7. Basic reading knowledge of the Greek language as demonstrated by the ability to translate from the first book of Homer's *Iliad* or from Plato's *Apology*.

8. Knowledge of grammar and syntax of classical Latin.

This group of professors also shaped the categories and their weights on the licensure test for prospective teachers of Latin and Classical Humanities in Massachusetts.

Multiple-Choice (100 items)		*Approximate Test Weighting*
I.	Reading Comprehension of Latin	15%
II.	Language Structures and Language Acquisition	25%
III.	Cultural Understanding	20%
Open Response (2 items)		
IV.	Integration of Knowledge and Understanding	20%

The PRAXIS II test for Latin teachers (0600) is similar in intellectual spirit but nowhere as demanding in scope. It contains 120 items.
They are divided into five categories and their weights are shown below.

Multiple Choice		Approximate Number of Questions	Approximate Percent of Examination
I.	Grammar	30	25%
II.	Reading Comprehension, Translation, and Literary Skills	48	40%
III.	Roman Civilization	18	15%
IV.	English Word Study, Derivatives, and Cognates	12	10%
V.	Pedagogy and Professional Matters	12	10%

The objectives for the test indicate that the content of the first section is
based on four to six authentic passages drawn from classical and later
Latin. But we are given few clues to specific authors. One poetic passage is to be by Vergil, Horace, Ovid, or Catullus, and one prose selection is to be by Cicero, Livy, Pliny, Caesar, Sallust, or Nepos. Who
might the authors of the other selections be? Why is recognized author-
ship important for only two of the passages?

LICENSURE TESTS FOR TEACHERS OF YOUNG STUDENTS

The licensure tests for teachers of young students, the group of tests
most needing revision in Massachusetts in 2000, were intended for
those seeking a license as Early Childhood, Elementary, or Special
Education teachers. The major questions we sought to address were:

(1) What academic subjects should generalists teaching young students be tested on and to what depth? (2) What should be expected academically of teachers of nursery through kindergarten children? (3) How should expectations change for elementary and special education teachers?

The major academic responsibilities for all three types of teachers are similar: teaching beginning reading, writing, and arithmetic, whether they teach kindergarten, grade 3, or learning disabled children. But how much can a multi-subject licensure test of 80–100 test items devote to beginning reading instruction in an effort to ensure adequate reading methods coursework in teacher preparation programs? A secondary issue (at the time) was the extent of mathematical knowledge to require in a revised test. In 2000, my staff and I were ready to tackle the first issue. To try to upgrade requirements for both reading and mathematics at once was sure to elicit opposition from the education schools and kill any attempt to increase academic requirements for aspiring elementary teachers.

Stand-Alone Licensure Tests of Reading Instructional Knowledge for Teachers of Elementary-Age Children

We decided to try for a stand-alone test for (eventually) all three groups of prospective teachers to make sure that what was known from a large, credible body of reading research (often called "scientifically based reading research") was adequately covered, but not to the exclusion of other important aspects of beginning reading instruction.[2] The original subject test for new elementary teachers (dated 1998) covered all subjects taught in a self-contained class including music, art, and physical education, as well as child development. It thus couldn't assess any one of the subjects adequately. Worse, the original subject tests for early childhood teachers and special education teachers did not assess any research-based knowledge of beginning reading instruction.

A stand-alone test of reading instructional knowledge meant a lot of test items in one area, on a new test, although prospective teachers would still have to take a subject test covering other major subjects in the curriculum. At a series of meetings across the state in the fall of 1999, we found general agreement that the original test for prospective teachers of elementary-age children did not assess beginning reading instructional knowledge adequately. Teacher education faculty also agreed that many children in Massachusetts were not learning how to read or read well. So they were willing to support a stand-alone licensure test of reading instructional knowledge in addition to a test of other areas of the elementary curriculum (i.e., two subject matter tests). No one complained that requiring a stand-alone test on reading instruction would be a financial or test preparation burden. We also found agreement that a reading specialist should know more than a classroom teacher and pass a different stand-alone test of reading instructional knowledge.

I was able to avoid sparking another round in the "reading wars" because of academic pushback against Whole Language's influence on an early draft of the English language arts standards in the 1990s. The commissioner had received a petition signed by 41 linguists and psycholinguists, most associated with MIT, to the effect that Whole Language was a fraudulent theory. Since the linguistics department at MIT could not easily be accused of being a sanctuary for right-wing extremists, the English language arts standards document had ended up with an appendix on the need to teach decoding skills. After getting a change in licensure regulations to indicate that passing a stand-alone test of reading instructional knowledge would henceforth be required for licensure, I drew on my own background in reading research and developed a draft outline of strands, sub-strands, and weights. I then asked two well-known and popular professors of reading, one in each "camp" (Whole Language/Balanced Literacy and Decoding Skills) to collaborate in revising my outline. I knew that both knew the research on beginning reading.

I promised that the outline they revised and sent back to me would go to a group of about 20 professors, specialists, and researchers on reading methods for further revision if deemed necessary. Their revised outline (which contained a few changes) went as promised to the larger committee for further revision; only a few changes were made at this point—the major one was moving the vocabulary sub-strand from the skills section to the reading comprehension section. (Everyone in the field by this time understood the process I was using and who was involved.)

The final revision then went out to the entire field in 2000 for comment. I read all feedback to ensure we were not omitting anything seen as important. The final version was used by another large committee of reading professors, specialists, and researchers for developing and reviewing test items. A battle in the "reading wars" had been avoided and we had a useful test.

The test (90) became operational in 2002.[3] It is by far the strongest one of its kind in the country—a claim based both on Massachusetts student scores on the NAEP reading tests in grades 4 and 8 and on the judgment of educators who know the research on beginning reading instruction. That was why the Connecticut Board of Education, at the recommendation of its commissioner of education, adopted the test in 2008 without any change in content and with only a slight change in the pass score. In April 2012, the Wisconsin legislature adopted the test; it was scheduled to have the same pass score in September 2014 as in Massachusetts. North Carolina's Board of Education adopted the test in December 2012 for implementation in 2014. According to a North Carolina newspaper, top officials at its Department of Public Instruction were told by Massachusetts officials that the Bay State "owed its success to this test" for the increase in student scores that put the state in first place in grades 4 and 8 on NAEP reading tests in 2005 and since then. New Hampshire's Board of Education adopted the test in 2013; it became operational in January 2014, with the same pass score as in Massachusetts.

Licensure Tests for Reading Specialists

The process used for developing a stand-alone test for prospective reading specialists (08) in the Bay State was similar to the process for developing 90 except that it started with the content of 90 as its blueprint. How different should it be? The major issue the test development committee wrestled with and worked out was the nature of the work to be done by someone called a "reading specialist." Was the license to be chiefly for a semiadministrator position (e.g., a director of reading) or for a clinician (e.g., a diagnostician) who would be able to do one-on-one work with children? The resolution of this issue would affect the weights on the test.

After much argument, the committee reached consensus that a license was needed for a clinician, not an administrator. Therefore the committee worked out weights for strands as well as the sub-strands and specific objectives. The distinction between these two stand-alone tests (and between the preparation programs leading to licensure as a teacher of reading or as a reading specialist) remains important even if the distinction is not observed in many state frameworks for teacher and specialist licensure or in the tests they take. We also required the preparation program for a Reading Specialist to take place at the graduate level—and built in a year of teaching experience as another requirement.[4]

Comparisons with other Licensure Tests for Elementary Teachers

Only a stand-alone test can adequately assess a prospective teacher's reading instructional knowledge and only if the test is long enough to include questions on each of the five major elements identified by the NRP.[5] All three licensure test companies provide such tests, but they are not identical in coverage of essential content.

ABCTE offers a stand-alone reading test that may be allowed in some states as an alternative to the required reading test for initial licensure of an elementary or special education teacher, although the test may be used most frequently as an endorsement in reading for an already-licensed elementary teacher. It is a relatively strong test of the basic elements of beginning reading instruction.

ETS offers several different tests assessing reading instructional knowledge. Reading Across the Curriculum: Elementary (0201) has 60 questions and three short essays, reissued in 2012. The vocabulary section includes word analysis and all the basic reading skills (phonics phonemic awareness, and print concepts), but accounts for only 17 percent of *half* of the test.

In 2012, ETS created a new PRAXIS II test: Elementary Education: Multiple Subjects (5031) that contains four separately scored sections, one of which is on Reading and Language. This section contains 60 test items, 32 of which assess reading instructional knowledge. This is far from being sufficient even if all 32 test items focus on research-based reading instructional knowledge. It is not clear from the PRAXIS website that all 32 do. Even if they did, 32 test items do not constitute an adequate assessment of reading instructional knowledge.

In 2013, ETS developed two other stand-alone PRAXIS II reading tests. Teaching Reading (5204) seems close in content to the Massachusetts Foundations of Reading Test (90) but is described as designed for "adding a reading endorsement to an existing license." It is further described as designed for "individuals whose preparatory program has included intensive training in the teaching of reading." About 36 percent of the test addresses "emergent literacy (oral language, concepts of print), phonological awareness, alphabetical principle/phonics, and word analysis." Vocabulary is worth another 14 percent. Comprehension and fluency are another 25 percent. "Instructional practices" are covered by three essay questions worth another 25 percent. However, test objectives do not make a clear distinction between imaginative/literary texts and informational/expository texts and the different elements in and skills needed for each major type of text, as indicated by the section of this test titled "Reading Comprehension Strategies across Text Types."

The second stand-alone test, Teaching Reading: Elementary Education (5203), is like 5204; it has 90 multiple-choice questions and three essay questions. But it is not clear from the ETS website for whom this test is designed or how its reading test items differ from those in 5204; it appears different chiefly because it has a section on how writing supports reading instead of a section on instructional practices. Like 5204, the test is described as reflecting the five essential components of effective reading instruction identified by the National Reading Panel. But, also like 5204, the test does not make a clear distinction between imaginative/literary texts and informational/expository texts and the different elements in and skills needed for each major type of text, as indicated in the section of this test titled "Reading Comprehension Strategies across Text Types."

This is the key challenge teachers of reading need to address in states that have adopted Common Core's standards, and the muddle in the Reading Comprehension section (E) of this test reflects the muddle in current reading methods coursework and the work of reading researchers themselves. The Massachusetts Foundations of Reading Test (90) makes a clear distinction between the two types of text, possibly a major reason for its increasing popularity across states.

Stand-Alone Licensure Tests of Reading Instructional Knowledge for Preschool Teachers

Should teachers licensed to teach very young children from birth to the primary grades be expected to pass a stand-alone licensure test on reading instructional knowledge expected of elementary teachers? The answer in Massachusetts was yes. The explanation has to do with changing children's needs. In by-gone times, children who attended nursery school and/or kindergarten were expected to spend most of their school time working on social skills—chiefly through play activities. This focus was fine for children of parents who read regularly to them, enriched their language through conversation and varied cultural activities, and cultivated number skills and logical thinking through card and board games.

For children whose parents did not supply this "hidden curriculum," and for the increasing numbers of children who did not acquire adequate reading, writing, and arithmetic skills in our public schools, it wasn't just the academic rigor of the early childhood curriculum that needed to be strengthened. Their teachers needed to learn much more than they once did in their preparation programs. Early childhood program directors were often reluctant to upgrade what these prospective teachers needed to know how to teach. A deeper problem was the spread of years covered by this license—a problem in many, perhaps most, states.

In most states today, this license often covers the first eight to ten years of a child's life. This enormously important period of years includes academic work in the primary grades that is inadequately addressed by a preparation program stressing child development, social skills, and play activities. Overly ambitious professional organizations and education school faculty have over the years converted what had once been a license for nursery school/kindergarten teachers into a license spanning the care of newborn infants to teaching demanding academic standards to ten-year-old children. The modest requirements once in place for the play-oriented kindergarten teacher are no longer adequate.

The Early Childhood license in Massachusetts went up to grade 3. After a prolonged battle inside and outside the department of education, I got coverage whittled down to grade 2. Undergraduate students in early education programs are in general the academically weakest link in the chain of prospective teachers for our public schools, yet they must develop beginning knowledge as well as basic academic habits and attention spans for formal schooling. Fortunately, education faculty in Massachusetts agreed that these prospective teachers should be required to take the same stand-alone reading test that prospective elementary teachers take. But, to date, nothing has been done to upgrade the depth and breadth of mathematical knowledge they should be assessed on in their other subject-oriented licensure test.

LICENSURE TESTS FOR TEACHERS OF MIDDLE SCHOOL STUDENTS

The middle school, like the junior high school it evolved from, has been an educational problem child ever since it was conceived. Were these middle years (grades 5–8) the culmination of the elementary school curriculum? Or were they the beginning of academic sequences in the five major subjects that would culminate in advanced coursework by the upper high school years (English, history, mathematics, science, and a foreign language)? The junior high school in name alone suggested a more academic orientation; at its inception, the middle school had more social than academic goals. Moreover, it introduced more variations in classroom organization than existed in the subject-divided junior high school day (typically grades 7–9) to accommodate its social orientation.

While there may be little difference in *curriculum* today between the two types of middle schools because of the equalizing effect of state standards on what is taught at each grade level, crucial differences developed in the *academic background* of the teacher for each structural type. The academic differences have probably had more influence on student achievement than the philosophical differences did, although there seems to be no research comparing the academic qualifications of today's middle school teachers with the academic qualifications of teachers in the old junior high school model.

In the junior high school model, teachers were typically expected to hold a secondary license for grades 7–12. Whether they did their student teaching at the junior high school or high school level, they were expected by a building principal to be capable of teaching the subject (or field) of their license at any secondary grade and to any group of students in the secondary grades. The academic expectation was usually an undergraduate major in the subject—or at the least a strong minor.

As the middle school concept began to sweep across a state (in Massachusetts, for example, there are only two junior high schools left), middle school advocates succeeded in getting generalist "middle school" licensure programs developed to accommodate their philosophy and structure. In addition, they developed a way for practicing teachers to become licensed as "middle school generalists." This mechanism (which may have begun earlier to enable teachers of one subject to become licensed to teach another subject) may have contributed more to lowering the academic level of the teacher who taught subjects in grade 7 or 8 than middle school preparation programs did because the majority of teachers licensed as middle school generalists may have obtained their license in this way. Clear data are not available to find out whether middle school teachers are more apt to have been trained as middle school teachers, as elementary teachers with an "added" license to teach up to grade 8, or as teachers with a K–8 license with an added "endorsement" to specialize in teaching one, some, or all subjects in the middle school.

Why was "adding" a license a popular route to middle school teaching? Probably because it was an easier way to get the number of legally licensed teachers needed for grades 5–8. The teachers licensed for 7–12 could not legally teach grades 5 and 6 unless they earned an elementary license (and did the necessary student teaching for it). It was much easier for elementary teachers who were already licensed to teach grades 5 and 6 to "add" a middle school license to teach grades 7 and 8 if requirements entailed taking only a course in adolescent development (and perhaps one or two survey courses in a subject taught in middle school). The academic content required for a middle school license was not excessively demanding. An undergraduate program could consist of a potpourri of courses across all major subject areas (maybe two in each area). A master's degree program for a middle school license also had a mix of courses. Such a light academic mix was deemed sufficient for teaching in the "cluster," "team," or whatever unit was created to serve as a transition from a self-contained elementary classroom to the subject-divided day of the senior high school.

School administrators in K–8 or 5–8 schools liked the flexibility of the middle school generalist license (for grades 5–8), especially in a rural state, in contrast to the single subject–licensed secondary teacher (for grades 7–12). But the academic limitations of the generalist in grades 7 and 8, in mathematics and science in particular, soon became apparent and the license was phased out in many states or not accepted (as in Boston, long before Massachusetts eliminated the license in 2000).

Licensure Tests for Middle School Teachers of Two Subjects

A compromise developed in some states, including the two-pronged plan my staff and I worked out in Massachusetts in 2000. The first prong consisted of offering two content-based middle school licensure tests, one for English and history, the other for science and mathematics, with the number of required academic credits equal to about two minors for each license. (Once a test becomes available, preparation programs can develop to address them.) These types of licensure tests were clearly more academically focused than the "generalist" test was. Although they could not go into the depth and breadth of either of the two subjects each one addressed, the teacher who held one was, other things being equal, academically preferable to the "glorified" elementary teacher who had added a middle school generalist license.

Licensure Tests for Middle School Teachers of a Single Subject

The second prong of the plan consisted of offering single-subject licenses in mathematics and general science for grades 5–8 only. These licenses were based on the need for more academically knowledgeable teachers in the middle school than the two-subject licenses were apt to produce. They reflected a kind of Hobson's Choice. Single-subject teachers licensed for 5–8 would not be as academically knowledgeable as the secondary teacher licensed for 5–12 or 7–12, but middle school principals would be more likely to find a mathematics or science teacher licensed for 5–8 than a mathematics or science teacher licensed for 5–12 or 7–12 (in other words, a mathematics or science major). Single-subject teachers licensed for 5–8 would not have to know as much as teachers licensed for 5–12, but they would be apt to know their subject better than the typical elementary school teacher.

Moreover, we expected prospective mathematics or science teachers who failed the 5–12 test but still wanted to teach mathematics or science to be able to pass the 5–8 test. The new test deliberately covered less mathematics and science than the test for 5–12 did and, as time showed, served its intended purpose. A large number of prospective teachers take and pass it. Because this single-subject middle school license restricts its holders (legally) to the middle school (which prevents them from moving up to the high school to teach), it safeguards the right of high school students to a qualified mathematics or science teacher. But because the test for the middle school mathematics or science teacher is easier than the licensure test for 5–12 or 7–12, it provides entry into teaching mathematics or science by a broader base of potential teachers.

We were able to determine the value of the middle school mathematics licensure test during the first year of its existence. It became available in September 2002 and was taken by 652 test takers in its first three administrations. (This test contains some items on calculus but addresses mainly algebra and geometry.) We were able to determine the number of test takers who had already failed the mathematics test for grades 7–12 before September 2002 and who took and passed the new middle school mathematics test in September 2002, November 2002, or February 2003. The pass rate was 70 percent and the state ended up with 98 more teachers qualified to teach middle school mathematics than it would have had without the test (assuming that those who failed once would likely have failed the secondary test for 7–12 again (retest pass rates in all subjects were and remain low). Thus, a middle school licensure program and test restricted to mathematics achieved the two goals we aimed for: (1) a supply of more knowledgeable middle school teachers of mathematics than the process of adding a middle school license to an elementary license led to, and (2) a larger supply of licensed teachers of mathematics for the middle school than the license for 7–12 or 5–12 would have led to.

Licensure Tests for Mathematics Teachers

The chief issue in listing topics in the regulations for the secondary mathematics teacher was how much mathematics one could reasonably require. Even in mathematics, where one might expect more consistency across colleges and states in the topics required in a mathematics major's coursework, there are many differences in what is required for both the major and for the minor. We also faced a Hobson's Choice here. Make the list of topics too demanding (i.e., rigorous) and one is not likely to get a prospective secondary mathematics teacher (i.e., anyone passing demanding coursework in these topics would likely go on to a high-paying position in industry or to graduate school in mathematics, physics, or a related area). Make the list of topics too undemanding to ensure a greater supply of high school mathematics teachers, and one would likely not have a high school mathematics teacher capable of teaching advanced mathematics (e.g., AB, never mind BC, calculus).

We compromised as we had with the requirements for prospective middle school mathematics teachers (discussed above) in order to ensure the possibility of competent mathematics teachers for middle schools. After conferring with several college-level mathematicians, we listed topics that would require study of algebra; trigonometry; discrete/finite mathematics; history of mathematics; abstract algebra; number theory; calculus through differential equations; probability and statistics; Euclidean, non-Euclidean, and transformational geometries; and applied mathematics or mathematics modeling. We were told this would ensure a mathematics teacher capable of teaching advanced placement courses, which are taught in many Massachusetts high schools.

While the topics look sufficiently demanding, the licensure test is a somewhat different matter. The weights were worked out by the review committee so that Number Sense and Operations was worth 12 percent; Patterns, Relations, and Algebra, 23 percent; Geometry and Measurement, 19 percent; Data Analysis, Statistics, and Probability, 10 percent; and Trigonometry, Calculus, and Discrete Mathematics, 16 percent. In other words, only 16 percent of the test addressed advanced mathematical knowledge. Another 20 percent covered two open-response questions. A test taker could probably get most of the advanced mathematics multiple-choice questions wrong but still pass the test because of where the pass score was likely set. Nevertheless, the pass rates in recent years hover around 70 percent of the test takers on the first try, and 50 percent or less of those retaking the test. A staff member who had been a summa cum laude mathematics major at a demanding liberal arts college estimated the level of difficulty of the test as a whole at about freshman college level—the hardest licensure test the state had developed, in her opinion. It is not clear why so many of the test takers who must think they can pass the test (otherwise, they would not take it) fail it.

LICENSURE TESTS FOR FULL-TIME MATHEMATICS TEACHERS IN THE ELEMENTARY AND MIDDLE SCHOOL

I had several mathematics tests for the lower grades developed: one for full-time elementary mathematics teachers, a combined middle school mathematics/science test (described above) for middle schools seeking someone who could teach both subjects, and a straight middle school mathematics test (also described above). All these tests were developed to ensure that elementary and middle school principals could hire new teachers who had more mathematics knowledge than typical elementary or middle school generalists had, but less knowledge than high school mathematics teachers would need.

The most successful (in terms of numbers taking/passing the test) was the middle school mathematics licensure test. The combined mathematics/science test didn't lead to large numbers taking/passing the test; I have been told that candidates could more easily pass the science portion (consisting of introductory courses across the sciences) than the mathematics portion. The elementary test was used more frequently (I was told) for the elementary mathematics coach position than the full-time elementary mathematics teacher. This use of the test assures that the coach knows more mathematics than the teachers he/she supervises, but it doesn't remedy the basic problem I sought to address: a mathematically inadequate elementary teacher in a self-contained classroom. That problem was solved several years later, as explained directly below.

STAND-ALONE LICENSURE TESTS OF MATHEMATICAL KNOWLEDGE FOR ELEMENTARY SCHOOL GENERALISTS

How much mathematics should prospective early childhood, elementary, and special education teachers know? Clearly, parents have good reason to think that these three groups of teachers should have a strong understanding of pre-algebra mathematics. They might well think these three groups of teachers already have this knowledge since they did complete elementary and middle school themselves—years earlier.

The Massachusetts Board of Education was the first state board to decide that a grasp of K–8 mathematics should be assessed on a stand-alone licensure test for prospective elementary and special education teachers, and in December 2006, it approved the development of such a test. Consisting of 40 test items, the test is based on the reasonable principle that these teachers-to-be should be expected to demonstrate, without the use of a calculator, a deep understanding of the mathematical concepts that underpin what they will teach their students, also without the use of calculators.[6]

The test went into effect in 2009. After a startlingly low pass rate (27 percent) on the first test administration, the pass rate has hovered around 50 percent on average over subsequent test administrations, suggesting how needed such a test was (only 60 percent of the items need to be correct for a passing score). The only opposition to the board's vote of approval for this pass score (in 2009) was from the state affiliate of the National Education Association. State affiliates of mathematics organizations approved it, and the one minority member of the board (at the time) indicated that academic quality came first, diversity second, in response to concerns expressed by other board members about the minority pass rate. There is no information available on what happens to test takers who never pass the mathematics portion of the test, no matter how many times they take it. The numbers who fail this test are very high.

To address the competition from the Bay State, ETS also developed a separately scorable mathematics test for prospective elementary teachers (also with 40 test items), available in 2011. It is too soon to find out the pattern of pass rates on this test, although pass rates are not easily comparable across states since states set their own pass score on a PRAXIS test.

The 40-item Massachusetts test of elementary mathematics knowledge in its General Curriculum test (03) and the 40-item PRAXIS test of elementary mathematics knowledge in its Multiple Subjects test (5031) are the only two stand-alone elementary mathematics tests available. But we do not know how strong the PRAXIS test is. The ETS website provides no information on how strong the test is or *who* developed the guidelines for test items on mathematics. In contrast, the mathematicians and others who developed the Massachusetts test are identified in *Guidelines for the Mathematical Preparation of Elementary Teachers.*[7] These 2007 guidelines also indicate what topics should be taught in mathematics coursework for prospective elementary teachers.

One may wonder why prospective special education teachers as well as elementary teachers were expected to pass the stand-alone reading and mathematics tests in Massachusetts. Since special education teachers are now apt to work side by side with the elementary teacher in many schools, it is reasonable to expect them to know as much about the major subjects taught in an elementary school curriculum as the teachers they work with—particularly since the licensure tests they have been required to take in many states have assessed no mathematics or reading instructional knowledge, while these are the two subjects most likely to need remediation or more teaching in learning disabled children.

LICENSURE TESTS FOR SCIENCE TEACHERS

I was fortunate to inherit from the 1994 regulations a relatively sound framework for secondary science licensure tests. As the National Council on Teacher Quality (NCTQ) put it, "Massachusetts does not offer certification in general science for secondary teachers, nor does it allow a combination of certifications, ensuring that any secondary level science teacher has passed a subject-matter test and is qualified in the specific area of science that he/she is teaching."[8] However, NCTQ could make that statement a few years ago only because in 2000 we took away the high school grade levels covered by the original General Science license (9–12) and pegged the license and existing test for only grades 5–8 or 1–6. I suspect most of those who pass it and teach in Bay

State schools teach in a middle school. All other science licensure tests were and remain specific to their subject (chemistry, physics, biology, earth science) and to the high school level. Relatively small numbers take these tests, and smaller numbers pass them.

To accommodate any possible interest by a middle school administrator in a teacher licensed to teach both mathematics and science, we developed a combined mathematics/science test, although relatively few people have taken the test, possibly because most middle schools want a full-time mathematics teacher and a full-time science teacher. The middle school science program has been popular, to judge by greater numbers taking and passing the middle school science test.

LICENSURE TESTS FOR TEACHERS OF COMMUNICATION AND PERFORMING ARTS

The issues that arose in working out the topics and test weights for prospective teachers of music, theater, and speech were similar to those I encountered in working out the topics for visual art and dance, fields whose tests I didn't have the opportunity to revise. One issue, which had also arisen in my attempt to address cultural competence through the regulations and tests for foreign language teachers, was how much weight to give to the literate or high culture in an art form. The second issue, analogous to an issue that had also arisen in working out topics for teachers of a foreign language, was the ahistorical nature of multicultural insistence on equal treatment of all cultural traditions in training communication and performing arts teachers for American public schools. The third issue was the negative effect of an affirmative action framework on the cultural range of test items test takers would encounter on one test and the possibility they could answer these test items correctly.

For Music Teachers

A licensure test for prospective music teachers in K–12 poses issues that relate as much to the precarious state of music education in our public schools as to its content. Depending on how strongly music education is supported in a community or state, a single license for K–12 in both choral and instrumental music may be the one license favored by music educators in a state. While it might be desirable in the abstract to prepare a music educator to be either a choral director or a band/orchestra conductor, the job market is such that a music educator with a single license for K–12 who can address both choral and instrumental music (and who has taken chiefly introductory courses in conducting, choral music, and instrumental music) is more attractive to school systems that can afford only one music educator and want a jack-of-all-trades more than a specialist. Music schools want their students seeking a position in the public schools to get a job, even if the student's interests and talents lie more in either vocal or instrumental music.

Once a state's music educators decide what type of license works best for them (in the Bay State it was the generic license for K–12), the delicate problem is working out topics for licensure requirements that do not negatively impact prospective teachers' preparation programs and that generate reasonable test items. A written test cannot capture how well a test taker sings, sight-reads, plays a keyboard, or conducts an instrumental group. The quality of a test taker's musical skills must be left up to the judgment of the music school faculty. Music schools have to have high standards for those they graduate because musical skills are audible to a layperson, and it is in the music schools' own interests to ensure that their graduates, if they go into the public schools as music educators, enhance the reputation of their training programs.

But music schools also don't want a gifted musician and a potentially good music teacher failing to get a license because the written questions pose unrealistic obstacles. Public schools can legitimately expect the music teachers they hire to be familiar with major composers and their works in musical history, to understand the nature of the instruments found in a typical school band or orchestra, to read standard musical notations on scores for a range of instruments even if they play their own instrument by ear, and to have some acquaintance with musical traditions other than our own. But there is a clear meaning to "our" for most music school faculty.

Music school faculty in Massachusetts (and the state is blessed with many fine music schools) indicated that the regulations and a licensure test should not require music students to know about every musical tradition in the world.[9] Music schools cannot offer coursework in every musical tradition in the world, multicultural test items are often trivial and/or obscure (e.g., the drumming patterns of West Nigerian drummers), test takers get many of these items wrong, and a normal four-year undergraduate schedule does not allow students time to take coursework on all musical traditions in the world, if such coursework even existed. In other words, music faculty find it unfair to be expected to address the multiculturalist demand, for licensure test purposes, that equal time be allocated to every musical tradition in the world. This was their chief problem with the original test for music educators (aside from a very high pass score).

This was similar to the implication that the foreign language college professors wanted to eliminate, to the effect that students of a language used by a 19th-century European empire would have to study every now-independent country using that language. The original licensure test for music educators expected, among other things, that test takers would be able to recognize "music from the major periods in music history and recognize characteristics, genres, and styles of American, Asian, African, and Hispanic vocal and instrumental music." In other words, an affirmative action framework was implicitly being imposed on the training of music educators, and an ignorant one at that—as if there is only one musical tradition in Asia, Africa, and South America, and as if Europe doesn't have any at all.

There is a definite Western base to what students need to study in music theory and musical history. As a result, I asked the music school faculty in Massachusetts to spell out, word by word, the language they wanted for the topics in the revised regulations (which affect their academic, not pedagogical, coursework and then the tests). Topics now include: "traditional Western music theory and harmony; music history and literature, including Western (European)—early Gregorian chant to present; and American music—1650 to present including ethnic folk, jazz, Broadway, and classic streams; and introductory knowledge of at least two other musical traditions with contrasting compositional and performance characteristics and genres."[10] About 33 percent of test weight is based on questions on music history, music literature, and aural analysis related to this literature. The message is clear: emphasis is on Western theory and musical history, and only two non-Western musical traditions need to be studied—and at a beginning level. So far as I know, music school faculty in Massachusetts are still satisfied with the licensure test that was revised in 2001 to address the topics they worded for the regulations.

For Theater Teachers

The various skills that prospective theater teachers need to acquire (e.g., acting, directing) are unlikely to differ much, if at all, across preparation programs and states. The knowledge that drama teachers should acquire, however, depends on how strongly those involved in writing objectives for a licensure field and test try to use an affirmative action framework for this knowledge. The revised regulations specify study of "American dramatic literature in the 20th century," "British, European, and classical Greek dramatic literature: historical periods, major stylistic traditions, major works and writers," and "history of drama," as well as "introductory knowledge of other world drama in its cultural and historical contexts." The only protest about requiring any content at all came from the head of the program preparing the most drama teachers in the state. Wouldn't prospective drama teachers acquire knowledge of relevant dramatic literature for an American public school from English courses? My reply: they probably would, but theater department faculty had to ensure that its students acquired that knowledge.

The acid test occurred when it came to distinctions and weights on the test. After prolonged negotiation, we arrived at a 25 percent weight for Theater History and Dramatic Literature, one-fourth of which was devoted to "British and other European dramatic literature from ancient times through the present," one-fourth to the "dramatic literature of the United States," and one-fourth to "dramatic literature from other cultural traditions." (The other one-fourth was the "history of drama and theater.") This was in contrast to the original 1998 test in which about 11 percent of the test items had to address drama and theater in American, African, Asian, and Latin American "cultures." The theater program now has to ensure that its students study some classical Greek, British, and other European dramatists and at least 6 percent of the test questions (over one-fourth of 25 percent) have to address classical Greek, British, and other European dramatic literature, which is the historical background to most of the plays a high school drama teacher typically has American students perform. Moreover, all 25 percent address knowledge of dramatic literature, not just skills.

For Dance Teachers

The 1995 regulations had lumped together several of the performing arts and spelled out only vague generalities for coursework in their preparation programs. For example, "The effective teacher of communication and performing arts" demonstrates knowledge of (among other things) "history, literature or criticism of dance, theater and communication within a world cultural context." Almost anything would fit into such a program. Although I didn't have the opportunity to revise the test itself, the regulations governing the content of dance programs were revised along the lines suggested for the music license by music school faculty. Dance programs would have to ensure their students learned, among other things, "history of Western dance performance, including historical periods, major stylistic traditions, and major artists; history of American dance performance from circa 1650; and introductory knowledge of dance traditions across the world."

For Speech Teachers

The amount of time spent in working out appropriate topics and objectives for a field and a test was rarely commensurate with the number of prospective teachers who would take the test and their job opportunities. The speech teacher was a prime example. The modern speech teacher is the professional descendant of the old elocution teacher of the 19th century and, in schools with one, is often the debating coach as well. Speech is a required course in all Texas high schools. It is a position that should be filled in every high school.

With the help of a professor of speech communication at a Boston-area university, we worked out a list of the topics that should be studied in an academic department by prospective speech teachers. The topics include "classical, modern, and contemporary theories of rhetoric"; "parliamentary procedure"; "important orations in American history"; and "history of the public speaking lecture circuits of the 19th century." It took time to work out topics in this area because there were few preparation programs for a speech teacher in the state and few speech teachers in the public schools. As a staff member discovered, the best debate coaches or speech teachers in the state, to judge by the high school students who won state or national competitions, were in private schools like Boston College High School and Milton Academy and could not participate on committees designed to work out appropriate topics and test items because the test developers were restricted to using public school teachers for peer input. As the situation now stands, the numbers taking the test are small and the numbers passing smaller yet.

For Visual Art Teachers

Again, while I did not have the opportunity to revise the original test, I did revise the topics in the regulations for preparation programs for Visual Art teachers to make them consistent with other performing arts. These topics included "major developments, periods, and artists in Western traditions in art and architecture; major developments, periods, and artists in American art and architecture from c. 1650 to the present; characteristics of art and architecture in two non-Western artistic traditions stylistically different from each other; influences of non-Western artistic traditions on Western art; and influences of Western art on non-Western artistic traditions."

It may not be clear to many readers yet, but these topics should be addressed in the academic coursework prospective art teachers take. These topics emphasize that prospective art teachers in American high schools should learn something about the major artists and architects in this country's history as well as the artistic heritage they drew on, in contrast to the vague requirement in the 1995 regulations that prospective art teachers demonstrate knowledge of "various cultural art heritages and the evaluations of civilizations," whatever the latter phrase means.

The licensure test based on the 1994 regulations was revised in 2010, but was not based on current regulations. Because the topics for the test were based on these 1994 regulations (which was illegal), art school faculty faced the same problem the music school faculty faced with the 1994 music test: they could not ensure that their students could address test items randomly generated about any of the 100 or more cultural traditions in the world. Sample items on the current Visual Art test range from questions about 19th-century Polynesian art and 16th-century Japanese art to 14th-century BCE Egyptian art—an incoherent cultural spread. Nothing on European artistic traditions.

The solution art school faculty and educators used to solve this problem was the one used by foreign language teachers in 2009 to cope with an excessive number of cultural traditions to expect prospective teachers to study—reduction of the number of questions (and the weight) for literate cultural competence. On the Visual Art test, they chose to allow about eight questions (10 percent of the test), in a section titled "Visual Art in Context," on "artworks from Africa, Asia, Central America, Europe, the Middle East, North America, Oceania, and South America." *And*, the objective includes "from ancient times through the twentieth century." Not surprisingly, they have achieved pass rates between 90–99 percent on most test administrations in recent years, in contrast to much lower pass rates on the original test. One may conclude that art school faculty in Massachusetts prefer to supply art teachers to the public schools who are relatively ignorant about all cultures rather than supply art teachers who are knowledgeable about the artistic heritage of the country supporting these schools. The more cultures multiculturalists discover, the less that can be learned and assessed about any one of them, even if a few have had far more influence historically than others.

LICENSURE TESTS FOR ENGLISH TEACHERS

What was once a cut-and-dried set of academic expectations for prospective English teachers is no longer true. The literary texts the public could expect a well-trained English teacher to be able to teach in a secondary class (e.g., Dickens's novels, Shakespeare's plays) are often not what that teacher ever studied as an English major, and the literary texts and/or authors they did study are often not what parents want them to teach in a public school. So, the state agency that determines the academic basis for a licensure test for English teachers cannot rely necessarily on whatever meets the requirements for an English major or leave it solely to a college English department to decide what a prospective English teacher for the public schools should study. The major criterion for selecting topics for a licensure test for English teachers was therefore what we, the staff, deemed was the appropriate background for teaching literature, language, and composition in a secondary classroom.

   This meant such topics as the principles of classical rhetoric, modern and contemporary theories of rhetoric, the history and structure of the English language, and the conventions for standard spoken and written English. For literature, we had to spell things out with detail so there would be no mistaking what would be assessed on a licensure test as well as expected in the academic coursework a prospective English teacher took. The two major literary topics read as follows: "American literature including the Colonial Period; the Revolutionary Period; American Romanticism and the American Renaissance (to include Hawthorne, Emerson, Melville, Whitman, and Thoreau); the Civil War and the postwar period; and fiction, poetry, drama from the early 20th century to the present." And "World literature including British literature (including the Anglo-Saxon period, the Middle Ages, the Renaissance, the Restoration and the 18th century, the Romantic Period, the Victorian Period, and the 20th century) and other European literature; literature of Africa, Latin America and Asia; Ancient Greek and Roman literature; the Bible as literature; world myths and folktales."

LICENSURE TESTS FOR HISTORY TEACHERS

Although Massachusetts provided for a license in history as well as in social studies before 2000, we found that most teachers teaching history in the state until the early 2000s were licensed as social studies, not history, teachers. The first step in addressing the limitations in the academic background of those teaching history at the middle and high school level was to abolish the social studies license. As a consequence, since 2000, the history or U.S. government teacher has had to be licensed as a history or government teacher for grades 5–8 or 8–12. [11]

   We faced the same dilemma in developing topics for prospective history (and U.S. government) teachers as we did for English teachers. We could not necessarily rely on what the education or academic faculty in the state's colleges and universities thought was the appropriate academic background for secondary history (and U.S. government) teachers, whether they majored or minored in history (or political science). The 1994 regulations had left academic preparation of prospective history teachers up to their college's requirements for a major. The wording in the 1994 regulations that had served as the point of departure for the original licensure test was the fatuous statement that the aspiring history teacher had to demonstrate knowledge of "methods of historical research; physical, economic, political, intellectual and social forces that shape civilizations, including gender, race and ethnicity; origin and development of world cultures; and the economic, political, social and cultural history of the United States." Even Renaissance Man would have been challenged to address all that. The purpose of such a broad statement, of course, was to allow almost anything for a major and for the licensure test.

As the music school faculty had done for the topics to be studied by a prospective music educator and to serve as the basis for a music licensure test, we spelled out what history teachers in an American public school needed to have learned in academic coursework in U.S. and world history, in addition to listing several broad objectives in geography, economics, and government. For U.S. history: "indigenous people of North America; European settlements and colonies; the American Revolution; expansion, reform, and economic growth of the United States up to the Civil War; the Civil War and Reconstruction; European immigration, industrialization, and scientific and technological progress; the two World Wars; and the United States from 1945 to the present." For world history: "human beginnings and early civilizations (Africa, Mesopotamia, Phoenicia, Egypt, India, China); roots of Western civilization (Israel, Greece, Rome); English and Western European history; Renaissance and the age of exploration; development of Asia, Africa, and South America; age of revolutionary change in Europe; the world in the era of two World Wars; and the world from 1945 to the present." What might have been taken for granted 30 years ago could no longer be taken for granted. Even then, this is hardly an airtight list of subtopics.

The final version of the topics went out in draft regulations for public comment by a vote of the board of education in mid-2000. While we could not know how many faculty members at the state's institutions of higher education actually read the list of topics a prospective history teacher needed to study, my staff and I read whatever comments we received in response to the public comment draft, and then decided whether and how to revise the topics (with a public rationale for whatever we did).

Once the draft regulations were approved (November 2000), the test company prepared an outline of the topics the prospective history teacher needed to study, together with a list of sub-objectives and weights for each topic. (This was done with all licensure tests, whether new or revised.) This outline served as the basis for generating items for the licensure test in history and, as with all the other outlines, it was distributed by the test company to all relevant education and academic faculty for comment. The test company later sent me a copy of all the comments it received, and before signing off, as I did on all proposed outlines, I had to judge whether the comments pointed to a needed correction. (For example, one person suggested ancient Egypt, not ancient Israel, as one root of Western civilization. Since this was historically incorrect, no change was made in the outline.)

The outline as well as the specific sub-objectives for the licensure test had to meet with general approval from the field for the test to be acceptable. This meant that relevant faculty had at least two opportunities to shape what a future history teacher would need to know to become licensed as a teacher of that subject. They could comment on the topics in the draft regulations and they could comment on the outline for the test itself. Whatever topics, therefore, are in the regulations for history (and for all the other fields discussed in this chapter) can be assumed to have met with overall approval by the relevant field and the Board of Elementary and Secondary Education (BESE).

So far as can be known, not only did the topics for study by a prospective history teacher meet with the general approval of the field (which is why they are in the regulations), so also did the outline of the history test, its sub-objectives, and its weights. As further support for our choice of topics in the regulations, we could later point to survey information from elementary and high school history teachers on the emphases they preferred for the state's History and Social Science Curriculum Framework, a document finalized in 2002.

In response to one survey I sent out, a majority of the hundreds of elementary teachers in the state signed with individual names (we required individual identification) to tell us if they preferred to teach about a range of ancient civilizations in K–5 or local, state, and U.S. history and geography. They made it clear they preferred the latter to the former, for at least two reasons. The latter topics were of greater relevance to their students inasmuch as the state has an abundance of historical sites and museums addressing American, British, black, and indigenous people's history (field trips to a local museum were always part of the elementary school curriculum) and they were of greater importance to the development of their students' identity as Americans.

In response to another survey I sent out, we received replies from about 1000 individual high school teachers about a preference for an emphasis on U.S. and Western history at the high school level and for a test of U.S., not world, history for the graduation requirement. This was a highly contentious issue at the time. The preference was for an emphasis on U.S. history.

The revised regulations and licensure tests made it clear what disciplines should be stressed by prospective teachers of history in their undergraduate coursework. Those seeking a history license for grades 5–8 or 8–12 now take a test with 37–39 items on U.S. history, 30–32 items on world history, and 30–32 items on geography, government, and economics (plus two short essays).

LICENSURE TESTS FOR U.S. GOVERNMENT TEACHERS

In many states, a course in U.S. government (or Civic Education or Problems in American Democracy) is required and is often taught in grade 12. In many high schools, a yearlong Advanced Placement course in U.S. and comparative government is also offered, and its first semester is usually U.S. government. Teachers of these courses are usually social studies or history teachers. Since we had just abolished the social studies license (as well as the middle school generalist license) when we began revising the licensing regulations, I had an opportunity to orient the academic background for the U.S. government teacher along the lines suggested by the Center for Civic Education's *We the People* program—toward political science and political philosophy. Both to attract students who major in political science, and to emphasize political philosophy, as did the *We the People* institutes, I merged these two phrases for the title of the license (i.e., political science/political philosophy). A few years ago, one of the state's teacher unions tried unsuccessfully to remove "political philosophy" from its title.

A licensed history teacher can also teach a U.S. government course because the academic topics in the regulations for approved preparation programs for both history and government teachers include "principles of American government," as do their licensing tests—meaning that coursework in these principles is required for an "approved program." (As noted by Benno Schmidt in a *Governance for a New Era: Blueprint for Higher Education Trustees*, "constitutional history" is a field "fast disappearing from college curricula.")[12] But the topics for U.S. government teachers specifically required moral or political philosophy. Topics include: founding documents of the United States and Massachusetts, American government and politics, comparative government, theories of political science or philosophy, and international relations. The government teacher needs to study geography and economics, as well as history. For the profile of the two licensure tests, we simply reversed the weights for history and government. In other words, both kinds of prospective teachers need to study political science, history, geography, and economics. The prospective history teacher would be encouraged to major in history, while a political science major might be encouraged to become a U.S. government teacher (instead of going on to law school or graduate work in international relations).

The test company produced a first-rate test for this license.[13] Topics from sociology, anthropology, and psychology as disciplines are not addressed on either licensure test, nor can teachers be licensed to teach these subjects in K–12.

NOTES

1. Sandra Stotsky with Lisa Haverty, "Can a State Department of Education Increase Teacher Quality? Lessons Learned in Massachusetts," in *Brookings Papers on Education Policy, 2004*, ed. Diane Ravitch (Washington, DC: Brookings Institution, 2004), 131–80.

2. Sandra Stotsky, "Why Reading Teachers Are Not Trained to Use a Research-Based Pedagogy: Is Institutional Reform Possible?," paper presented at the Courant Institute of Mathematical Sciences, New York University, October 2, 2005. http://www.google.com/search?ie=UTF8&oe=UTF8&sitesearch=www.nychold.com&q=sandra+stotsky&btnG=Search&domains=www.nychold.com.

3. The report by the National Reading Panel (NRP) came out in late 2000, but too late to influence the development of the Massachusetts test. That is

why some terminology in the test is not identical to terminology in the NRP report. ("Fluency," a major term in the NRP report, is implied by "automatic" or "rapid" word recognition, but the term was not used in the regulations or the test.) Nevertheless, even though the Massachusetts test was not based on NRP's recommendations, it was compatible with them because many reading researchers and specialists in the Bay State were familiar with the results of reading research, some of which, in vocabulary, goes back almost 100 years.

4. Almost all those licensed as Reading Specialists come from dedicated master's level programs. What is puzzling is that the pass rate for first-time test takers is not very high—about 55 percent. It is puzzling because one would expect a dedicated master's level program to be strong enough (and its entry bar to be high enough) so that most of its completers would pass the culminating licensure test for the program. On the other hand, the penalty for not passing the test for Reading Specialist is a minor one—the test taker does not get a license to work as a Reading Specialist. The test taker still gets a M.Ed. in reading and thus may earn a salary step and/or a promotion to district administrator of reading programs. The test taker can also continue to teach in a classroom. Failing this licensure test is not like failing a reading test for elementary or special education licensure, which prevents (in theory) the test taker from teaching in any classroom. ETS provides two tests for Reading Specialist. One test (0300), reissued in 2008, provides minimal coverage of foundational reading skills. Its largest section has 54 questions weighted as 45 percent of the test. The other, 0301/5301, is a new test with 80 multiple-choice questions and two open response questions. It appears to cover basic reading skills far more extensively than 0300, and in its overall categories and weights bears a close resemblance to the Massachusetts Reading Specialist test (08).

5. Sandra Stotsky, "Licensure Tests for Special Education Teachers: How Well They Assess Knowledge of Reading Instruction and Mathematics," *Journal of Learning Disabilities*, September/October 2009, 42(5), 464–74. http://ldx.sagepub.com/cgi/content/abstract/42/5/464; Sandra Stotsky, "Why American Students Do Not Learn to Read Very Well: The Unintended Consequences of Title II and Teacher Testing," *Nonpartisan Education Review*, 2006, 2(1). http://www.npe.ednews.org/Review/Articles/v2n1.pdf.

6. Sandra Stotsky, "How State Boards of Education Can Upgrade Math Teaching in the Elementary School," *National Association of State Boards of Education (NASBE) Newsletter*, February 2007, 13(2).

7. *Guidelines for the Mathematical Preparation of Elementary Teachers*, Massachusetts Department of Education. http://www.doe.mass.edu/mtel/mathguidance.pdf.

8. National Council on Teacher Quality, "The All-Purpose Science Teacher: An Analysis of Loopholes in State Requirements for High School Science Teachers," 2011, 6.

9. Sandra Stotsky, "Who Should Be Accountable for What Beginning Teachers Need to Know?," *Journal of Teacher Education*, 2006, 57(3), 256–68. http://jte.sagepub.com/ andhttp://JTE.sagepub.com/content/vol57/issue3.

10. Massachusetts Department of Education, Regulations for Educator Licensure and Preparation Program Approval, 603 CMR 7.00, June 2003, p. 27.

11. As of this writing, teachers licensed to teach history at the high school level in Massachusetts must have passed the history test for grades 8–12 (and could have majored in history or political science), while teachers licensed to teach history at the middle school level must have passed the same history test or a middle school test in English and history for grades 5–8 (for a middle school humanities license).

12. Benno C. Schmidt, *Governance for a New Era: A Blueprint for Higher Education Trustees* (Washington, DC: American Council of Trustees and Alumni, 2014), 8.

13. The test contains 18–20 items on political philosophy, 24–26 items on U.S. government and civics, 18–20 items on comparative government and international relations, 24–26 items on history, and 11–13 items on geography and economics (as well as two short essay questions).

7

OTHER FACETS OF A TEACHER LICENSING SYSTEM TO STRENGTHEN

Revising current teacher licensure tests and developing new tests are not the only changes to make to a state's licensing system to strengthen the academic background teachers bring to the curriculum they teach. Other less visible aspects of the regulatory system also need attention. These include the following:

1. Prospective teachers' undergraduate major,
2. Academic time on task in the undergraduate program,
3. Useless or outdated licenses,
4. Grade levels covered by a license,
5. Grade levels and practicum hours required for student teaching, and
6. Types of test items on licensure tests.

Below is a brief explanation of these facets of a licensing system and what we did (or tried to do) about them in each area in the revised 2000 teacher licensing regulations in Massachusetts.

UNDERGRADUATE MAJORS

Before prospective teachers could be awarded an initial license, MERA required them to earn a bachelor's degree from an accredited institution of higher education, with a "major in the arts and sciences appropriate to the instructional field." After 1993, prospective teachers could not have an education major unless it was a second major, something that some colleges in Massachusetts require of undergraduates seeking a teaching license. By law their primary major has to be in the arts and sciences.

The requirement of an arts and sciences major was intended to ensure that prospective teachers take some demanding upper-level courses in the arts and sciences, in addition to arts and sciences electives or distribution requirements. Education as a "major" (still possible in many states) was and remains an intellectually flat major because there is little academic coursework after the sophomore year.

But the requirement of an appropriate arts and sciences major didn't always solve the problem legislators sought to address, especially for aspiring elementary or special education teachers. After collecting information from those in charge of elementary or special education licensure programs, we found three different patterns for fulfilling the requirement of an arts and sciences major that violated the spirit of the statute: (1) a traditional but irrelevant major such as sociology, anthropology, or psychology—often the easiest major the undergraduate could find at her college, I was told; (2) a "grievance" major such as ethnic or women's studies; or (3) a composite major, an artificially constructed major that varies from college to college. It has many good things in it—a little of everything—but not much of any one thing. It is not one of the traditional majors at a college and probably results from collaboration between education faculty and arts and sciences faculty. In a well-intentioned attempt to provide prospective elementary (and sometimes middle) school teachers with some academic preparation in all the subject areas they teach, members of both faculties cobble together a few arts and sciences courses in each subject area taught in an elementary or middle school, join them to some education courses, and approve the camel as an arts and science major. This major has legitimate breadth but no intellectual depth. It may be deceptively called a "liberal arts" major.

In requiring an arts and sciences major for prospective teachers, legislators also hoped to curb the number of education courses undergraduates took to satisfy degree requirements. However, there is no evidence that this requirement had any effect on the amount of education coursework taken by undergraduates enrolled in a teacher licensure program who have to satisfy the requirements for their major and a bachelor's degree program as well. That is, there is no evidence a major in the arts and sciences reduced the number of education courses they took—if not for their education major if they were required to have one as a second major, then for their teacher licensure program. Either way, education faculty would get enrollment in whatever coursework they deemed their licensure programs should require.

Nor is there any evidence that the department's verbal efforts to recommend "appropriate" majors for prospective elementary teachers or, conversely, to discourage majors of little value for the subjects they would teach, led to more choices of a stronger major. Indeed, my own efforts met with fierce opposition from some education faculty in the state, with one accusing me of trying to deprive students at her elite college of their "academic freedom." However, the relatively high pass rates for prospective elementary teachers on their subject area tests today (except in mathematics) may signal stronger academic backgrounds; one dean of a small teacher training college told me personally of its successful efforts to steer students away from becoming psychology majors.

ACADEMIC TIME ON TASK

Because there were so many ways the demands of an undergraduate licensure program could eat away at the academic education of students simultaneously seeking a liberal arts education, we decided to spell out a specific number of semester hours for the academic coursework serving as background for the subject(s) taught by three different groups of teachers.

In the regulations approved by the state's Board of Education in the early 2000s, all prospective teachers of elementary and special education students were required to take "at least 36 hours in upper and lower level arts and sciences coursework covering composition; American literature; world literature including British literature; U.S. history from colonial times to the present; world history, including European history, from ancient times to the present; geography; economics; U.S. government including founding documents; child development; science laboratory work; and appropriate mathematics and science coursework." These prospective teachers were also to take a general licensure test addressing these subjects as well as a test addressing the fundamentals of beginning reading pedagogy.

The regulations in the early 2000s also sought to spell out academic time on task for prospective middle school teachers. Undergraduates seeking a middle school license to teach two subjects in grades 5–8 were required to take "at least 36 semester hours in a mathematics/ science or English/history program of studies." Department staff and I had originally proposed 48 hours (24 for each subject, or 6 courses at four credits per course for each), but had to compromise at the insistence of the then president of Lesley University, who complained to the commissioner of education that such academic demands would affect enrollment in its middle school licensure program. For those seeking a general science license, the requirement was at least 36 hours addressing the topics listed for the general science license.

As of 2014, all these requirements for "academic time on task" are gone from the regulations. When they were dropped is not clear. It may have been some time in 2010, according to an endnote on when this part of the document was amended. The bottom line is likely a weaker academic background for the elementary and middle school teachers who completed an undergraduate program in recent years.

WEEDING OUT OUTDATED LICENSES

Just as public libraries must "weed" their collections on a routine basis to make room for new acquisitions and remove outdated holdings (e.g., cookbooks, travel books), a system for teacher licensing also needs "weeding." We eliminated four licenses on academic grounds: the social studies license, the middle school generalist license, the home economics license, and the K–8 license.

The social studies license was eliminated in order to strengthen teachers of history, government, geography, and economics. Henceforth, those interested in teaching social studies in K–12 would have to earn a discipline-based license in history or political science/philosophy, and then take a licensing test that included topics in all four subject areas.

We eliminated the middle school generalist license because the preparation programs that had been developed to lead to this license typically required little more than a smattering of academic coursework across all the subjects taught in a typical middle school. It had come into being as a way to address what many educators perceived as the special needs of young adolescents when middle schools began to replace junior high schools across the country. Desperate middle school administrators needed a generalist license to address staffing holes in grades 5–8 or 6–8 and had been able to place academically underqualified teachers with this license in grades 7 and 8.

Only one licensure program in the state prepared students for the home economics licensing test; no more than a handful of students wanted what was perceived as an outdated license, and few if any schools hired for such a position any more. The program was merged into one with greater demand—Health/Family and Consumer Sciences. The K–8 license, also, was no longer wanted, even in rural Massachusetts schools.

GRADE LEVELS COVERED BY A LICENSE

The number of grades covered by a license, that is, the scope of a license, is a far more important feature of a license than non-educators realize. The specific grades covered by a license not only determine the educational level of the student-teaching experience but also influence how many and what kind of academic courses they take.

To ensure stronger academic backgrounds for teachers at specific grade levels, we made some changes in the grades covered by a license. The range of grades allowable for the early childhood license was reduced from pre-K–3 to pre-K–2, making grade 3 teachable by only a teacher with an elementary license (1–6). The range of grades allowable for middle school licenses was reduced from 5–9 to 5–8, making grade 9 teachable by only a teacher with a high school license. Correspondingly, the range of grades covered by a high school license was broadened from 9–12 to 8–12, so that teachers with the strongest academic background (those licensed to teach grade 12) could teach grade 8 if need be. In addition, grades 9–12 was eliminated from the general science license, which now addresses only grades 5–8. All prospective high school science teachers in undergraduate licensure programs hence-forth would have to take enough coursework in a particular science so that they could pass a discipline-specific test for licensure and teach that particular science with adequate depth in grades 9–12.

GRADE LEVELS AND PRACTICUM HOURS FOR STUDENT TEACHING

It was also necessary to be more specific about what grade levels a prospective teacher should do her student teaching in and the number of hours required for the "practicum" in order to be better prepared academically for the kind of school population she might end up teaching. For example, we required the aspiring Early Childhood teacher to have 300 hours altogether, but 200 of these hours had to be in grades 1–2, even though the majority of them would become kindergarten teachers.

We increased practicum hours for prospective elementary teachers. A next step would have been to require them to divide their student teaching between each of two grade spans (1–4 and 5–6) and between suburban and urban schools (something still not in regulations by 2014). Prospective elementary teachers do not tend to student teach as often at the highest elementary grades as at the lower grades. Nor are they required to student teach in both urban and suburban schools. If they were, they would be exposed to a wide range of students at the beginning and end of the elementary years and understand the spread in reading skills much better than they now do.

CONSTRUCTION AND TYPES OF TEST ITEMS ON LICENSURE TESTS

Even the construction and kinds of test items on the licensure tests needed attention. After inspecting a range of test items on tests for prospective teachers in K–8, I held a meeting with editors from the testing company. I did not want pedagogy to be tested on subject area tests, and the format of test items needed to promote abstract or deductive thinking on academic concepts, not situational or practical thinking on matters of pedagogy. As a result, both the new and revised tests are generally more intellectually demanding than the original tests (according to the president of NES). In addition, the testing company was willing to spend more time in trying to recruit more arts and sciences faculty for the committees charged with reviewing test objectives and test items.

8

STRENGTHENING VETERAN TEACHERS

The Massachusetts Education Reform Act (MERA) of 1993 wanted to upgrade veteran teachers as urgently as it intended to upgrade prospective teachers by means of tests of their academic skills and knowledge and by holding their preparation programs accountable for the results. In addition to strengthening programs and requirements for prospective teachers, we therefore needed to work out regulations that would strengthen already-licensed teachers. There were two groups of such teachers. The first group consisted of those who had received a beginning (Initial) license and could teach up to five years while seeking to meet requirements for the second and final license (Professional). The state already had a two-stage licensure process. The other and much larger group of teachers consisted of veteran teachers—those who were deemed by MERA in 1993 to have a Professional license and who needed to renew their license every five years.

For the first group of teachers, we concentrated on the requirements for a master's degree in education because that was and remains the easiest way for a newly licensed teacher coming from an undergraduate licensure program to receive full licensure. For the second group of teachers—arguably the most important group of teachers to reach in the state—we had no choice but to focus on professional development. We wanted to try to ensure that whatever professional development they received was of intellectual benefit to them and would contribute to the number of "professional development points" they needed for each five-year renewal of their license (a cycle mandated by MERA).

This chapter describes our efforts to strengthen the academic background of both newly licensed and veteran teachers. But first, a bit of history is useful for understanding the huge increase in the education coursework required in Massachusetts of prospective and licensed teachers in the past 70 years and a corresponding decrease in the academic coursework they took. This history suggests why state legislators were concerned about the academic quality of the state's teaching corps.

GRADUAL EXPANSION OF REQUIRED CREDIT HOURS IN EDUCATION COURSEWORK

Each state has a somewhat different history in licensing teachers but the overall trends are probably similar. It wasn't until 1956 that the Massachusetts legislature mandated licensure for all teachers. At the time, state regulations required only 12 credits in education courses including student teaching for an "approved program." After the 1982 revision of the regulations, a minimum of 21 credits in education courses plus student teaching was required.[1] The total number of credit hours that the institutions themselves required in their undergraduate teacher preparation programs was usually much more than the state minimum, although it varied widely within an institution for different licenses and across institutions for the same license. Whatever the number of credit hours, it eventually became a significant portion of the total number of credit hours toward a bachelor's degree.

In 1993 MERA required an arts and sciences major for prospective teachers (ending a solo education major), although it did not rule out the possibility of two majors, one of which could be an education major. In 2002, we surveyed all teacher preparation programs in the state to find out how many credit hours were required in these programs. We found that the percentage of total credits required in education coursework (including student teaching) as part of the total credits required for a bachelor's degree ranged (across institutions) from 16 percent to 39 percent in foreign languages, from 13 percent to 39 percent in science, from 13 percent to 42 percent in mathematics, from 22 percent to 51 percent in elementary education, and from 25 percent to 59 percent in special education. This meant that many newly licensed teachers coming from an undergraduate licensure program could not have acquired a strong background in the arts and sciences.

Once newly licensed teachers begin teaching, the lack of a strong foundation in the arts and sciences has been compounded by the absence of requirements that might in some way address a limited academic education. The salary schedule in most school districts in the country has rarely, if ever, made a distinction between a master of arts or master of sciences degree (M.A. or M.S.) and a master in education degree (M.Ed.), and the latter is much, much easier to obtain with respect to both the content and convenience of the coursework. Schools of education regularly offer late afternoon or weekend courses, and many also provide credit-bearing coursework in teachers' own school districts.

Few teachers who complete undergraduate licensure programs take graduate coursework in the subjects they teach and complete master's degrees in the arts and sciences. In a national survey of high school English teachers in grades 9, 10, and 11, I found that about one-third have an M.A. degree in English or the arts and sciences.[2] Today, most teachers get a master's degree in education (if they get one at all), whether they teach a core subject or are generalists (as are elementary and special education teachers).[3] It seems to matter little to school administrators or school boards that the coursework for a master's degree in education may be totally unrelated to the subject(s) taught by a teacher, and mind-numbing if not mindless.

For veteran teachers, the criteria for eligible professional development credits (for a salary schedule or license renewal) rarely, if ever, have made a distinction in quality and credits earned between attendance in a pedagogical seminar and participation in a discipline-oriented seminar. Moreover, opportunities to earn professional development credits have arisen in the teacher's own school in an expanding variety of ways—from serving on curriculum revision committees to attending in-service presentations on hot button social problems. While all may be legitimate activities for earning professional development credits, they rarely serve to deepen teachers' knowledge of their own discipline.

REQUIRED COURSEWORK FOR A MASTER'S DEGREE PROGRAM IN EDUCATION

The most contentious change we made in the 2000 regulations was to the content of the master's degree program in education for licensed teachers. This is the degree that the vast majority of licensed K–12 teachers in most states complete in order to achieve a second stage of licensure and/or a salary increase. The 2000 regulations specified that at least half of the courses in the master's degree program in education for licensed middle and high school teachers had to be in the arts and sciences, not in an education school, and had to be related to the subject area of the license. This may sound like common sense, but it was contested at the time both openly and behind the scenes.

In the 2014 version of the Massachusetts licensing regulations (on the Department's website), our efforts to upgrade the academic competence of licensed secondary school teachers (especially those in the middle school) are gone. The requirements for some coursework in the arts and sciences are no longer there. When these requirements (for the second stage of licensure) were dropped is not indicated, although it is likely that they were in effect for almost a decade. Why were they dropped? My guess is that education schools and the union to which most of their faculty belong probably did not want any master's programs coursework restrictions that meant a lower enrollment in education courses.

There had also been a huge increase in "graduate" coursework in education after passage of MERA in 1993. Although MERA required prospective teachers to have a major in the arts and sciences, it did not place any limits on the education coursework that teacher preparation programs could require for either the Initial or the Professional license. And it encouraged teachers to complete a master's degree program without specifying where that program should take place.

One might ask why this matters. It turns out that there is some research showing that having a master's degree in a subject (not in education) is related to student achievement (especially in mathematics and science). The most recent review of relevant research can be found in Matthew Di Carlo's review on the Shanker Blog.[4]

The correct classification of these master's degrees has eluded most researchers trying to determine how student achievement is affected by teachers earning a master's degree. Most studies have not distinguished a general master's degree in education *for already-licensed teachers* from a master's degree in education leading to licensure (also called an M.Ed.) and a master's degree in the arts and sciences in the subject the teacher teaches or majored in (the two may differ). These various master's degrees differ from the M.A.T. degree (a master of arts degree in teaching) that may be under the auspices of either the arts and sciences or the education school. This master's degree originally required an equal division between coursework in education and coursework in the arts and sciences (and was proposed in the 1930s by James B. Conant, then president of Harvard University). It was intended for completion of a postbaccalaureate teacher preparation program for able graduates of liberal arts colleges. The M.A.T. degree program today, where it still exists, differs in its requirements across institutions.

For the 2000 licensing regulations in Massachusetts, we could not touch the question of what kind of master's degree program an increase in the salary schedule in a school district should be based on. We simply reasoned that if already-licensed teachers wanted to earn a master's degree for the second stage in licensure (other options had to be available by law), it was of benefit intellectually to them as well as to their students to earn a master's degree that included pedagogical or academic coursework in the subject they taught.

My intent to upgrade the content of the master's degree in education for already-licensed teachers was motivated by an examination of the education coursework that had counted toward a general master's degree program in education. I had perused anonymous transcripts from the licensing office at the Department and was surprised by how few courses in these degree programs were related in any way to the subject(s) and grade levels taught by the teacher. An accumulation of credits from a random assortment of courses was all that these "programs" consisted of, in many cases.

REQUIREMENTS FOR PROFESSIONAL DEVELOPMENT

Two documents indicate how we sought to upgrade veteran teachers: *Recertification Guidelines for Massachusetts Educators*, dated January 2000, and *Guidelines for Professional Development Providers*, dated

February 2000. In these documents we followed up on what the Board of Education at that time had decided in December 1999—to "raise the standards for knowledge in the content area; provide an incentive for educators to engage in advanced academic study; . . . and establish a state registry of professional development providers." In an attempt to prevent educators from participating in frivolous or irrelevant professional development, a built-in safeguard was the requirement for supervisor approval indicating that 80 percent of the "professional development points" acquired for license renewal in each five-year cycle were "consistent with the educational needs of the school district."

The *Recertification Guidelines for Massachusetts Educators* spelled out how many points could be awarded for every conceivable kind of professional development we could conjure up. In every five-year cycle, at least 80 percent of these points had to come from professional development based on the content or pedagogy for the field of their license.

The *Guidelines for Professional Development Providers* listed the criteria for allowing professional development programs to award credits. It also provided an application form for those professional development providers who were not exempt from registration. However, colleges and universities, public school districts, charter schools, and educational collaboratives were exempt. Since these entities provide much of the professional development given to teachers, it is not clear how effective this or any registry could be. For the free workshops funded by the Department itself (using grants from federal and other sources), we required the involvement of academic experts in their design and delivery.

These criteria and requirements may well have raised teachers' consciousness about the importance of the academic base of their licenses, increased providers' efforts to include relevant academic content in their workshops, and improved teachers' academic knowledge. But it was not possible for us to do the kind of research that could determine to what extent these criteria and requirements stimulated teachers to pursue further academic study in institutions of higher education or contributed to a higher quality of professional development that benefited both the teachers and the students they taught.

CONCLUDING REMARKS

To judge by the little research that has been done, although the benefits of professional development for veteran teachers are not clear, nevertheless this country spends an enormous amount of money on professional development (for administrators as well as teachers). The implicit goal is to help veteran teachers learn to a large extent what they should have learned in their undergraduate years and in a master's degree program: the content of the subjects they are licensed to teach. (Many countries require subject area teachers in K–12 to complete a master's degree in their subject area before they can enroll in a teacher preparation program.) One possible solution to these related problems is for school boards to reward teachers (especially core subject teachers) more highly for earning a master's degree awarded by the arts and sciences faculty for coursework in an academic discipline than for a master's degree awarded by school of education faculty for pedagogical coursework. Coursework for an M.S. or M.A. degree is far more intellectually demanding than for an M.Ed. degree.

Core subject teachers should be offered a monetary incentive to take authentic graduate courses in their discipline or in related arts and science coursework rather than content-empty courses in a degree program in education—with expenses reimbursed by their districts, if not the state. This policy should be worked out via collective bargaining with the local teachers union.

Astute philanthropists could also step in and pay the fees that leading scholars, scientists, and other professionals command for preparing and giving suitable talks to school teachers on intellectual or artistic work in their discipline. Most teachers would be far more eager to attend a talk on American history by David McCullough or Gordon Brown or a poetry reading by Helen Vendler or Robert Pinsky in their school district than a workshop on school violence given by an up-to-date educational entrepreneur—the more likely kind of (expensive) in-service presentation arranged for teachers.

These suggestions would cost much less than the staggering costs we lay out today for remediation of our teaching corps through something misleadingly called "professional development." What would be costly is the courage needed by educational policy makers to tell the public why so many teachers are academically underqualified and need so much "professional development."

The greatest opposition would likely come from two sources: the education schools and the hordes of professional development providers that swarm over our K–12 schools. Education schools have a major grip on teacher training despite all the accelerated routes that states have made available for those who want to teach in K–12 without going through a lengthy pedagogy-based licensure program. Indeed, if anything, educators loudly advocate for more education coursework for prospective teachers, not more arts and science coursework, when we have no evidence from impartial research that education coursework leads to more effective teachers than academic coursework does.

Education school faculty would be joined in their opposition to more academic coursework for prospective teachers by the army of educational entrepreneurs now providing professional development. The latter make their living providing remedial programs in reading, mathematics, history, and science to the academically underqualified teachers whom the education schools regularly pass on to the nation's public schools. Each source of opposition is highly unlikely to permit changes that would reduce the size of their captive audience.

A giant step forward could be achieved by one relatively simple policy. State legislatures could eliminate undergraduate licensure programs overnight by removing all credit for undergraduate education coursework. By enabling them to have a full four years of academic coursework, this policy would immediately address the impoverished academic education that most undergraduates intending to be core subject teachers now receive. And a one- to two-year postbaccalaureate teacher preparation program culminating in a master's degree would enable them to begin teaching at a higher salary and without any need to spend some of their time on coursework for such a degree.

Would there be a teacher shortage? We already have one in key subjects: mathematics, science, and foreign languages. But we would be unlikely to have a shortage in other areas, as we already prepare many more elementary and early childhood teachers than we can employ.

NOTES

1. Personal communication from Margaret Cassidy, Program Approval Co-ordinator for Educator Preparation in Higher Education at the Massachusetts Department of Education from 1981 to 2005, with assistance from Judy Sohn-White, Coordinator for the Massachusetts Tests for Educator Licensure at the Department.

2. See Table E6 in Sandra Stotsky, *Literary Study in Grades 9, 10, and 11: A National Survey, FORUM* 4 (Boston: The Association of Literary Scholars, Critics, and Writers, Spring 2010), 17.

3. Having a master's degree can make a big difference in a teacher's salary. For example, as of 2006 in Brookline, Massachusetts, a teacher with just a B.A. degree earns $41,065 the first year, $43,318 the second year, $45,570 the third year, and $47,816 the fourth year. A teacher with a master's degree earns $43,784 the first year, $46,105 the second year, and $50,751 the third year. A third-year teacher with a master's degree thus earns much more than a fourth-year teacher with only a B.A. degree. As soon as a teacher earns a master's degree, the teacher's salary schedule moves from the first set of increases to the second set.

4. Matthew Di Carlo, "Research and Policy on Paying Teachers for Advanced Degrees," Shanker Blog, September 2, 2014. http://shankerblog.org/?p=10421.

9

STUDIES OF PREDICTIVE VALIDITY AND CONSTRUCT VALIDITY

From the time teacher tests were first developed, education researchers have tried to link teachers' test scores to their students' achievement. Below are brief descriptions of seven recent studies and what their authors claim they found. I then explain why their findings do not tell us much.

EXAMPLES OF STUDIES ON PREDICTIVE VALIDITY

In a 2006 study, Joshua Boot compared value-added results for 55 Tennessee teachers in self-contained elementary classrooms who took both ABCTE's multiple subject test for elementary teachers and its test of professional teaching knowledge.[1] Students of the 13 teachers who passed both ABCTE tests had significantly greater overall improvement in achievement than students of the other teachers (who failed to pass one or both of the ABCTE tests), exceeding one year's progress in all subjects. In other words, teachers who met ABCTE's requirements for elementary education certification produced greater academic achievement in their students, especially in mathematics, than teachers who did not. It should be noted that Tennessee's elementary teachers must pass several PRAXIS tests to obtain licensure.

In a 2007 study, Joshua Boot compared value-added results for 78 Tennessee middle school teachers (65 held secondary mathematics licenses, the others held apprentice or interim licenses) who took both ABCTE's secondary mathematics test and its test of professional teaching knowledge.[2] Students of the teachers with scores on the ABCTE secondary mathematics tests that were one standard deviation above the study mean showed greater gain in mathematics achievement than students of the teachers with scores that were one standard deviation below the study mean.

In a 2006 study, Dan Goldhaber analyzed the relationship between the quintile status of almost 24,000 North Carolina teachers on two PRAXIS tests they had taken for elementary licensure (PRAXIS 0011 and PRAXIS 0012) over a 10-year period (1994–2004) and the scores of their 701,000 students in grades 4 to 6 on state tests in mathematics and reading. His results "generally support the hypothesis that licensure tests are predictive of teacher effectiveness, especially in teaching mathematics."[3]

However, Goldhaber expressed concerned about "false positives" and "false negatives" in relation to the pass score that a state uses and considers current teacher tests a "weak signal" of teacher quality.

In a 2006 study, Charles Clotfelter, Helen Ladd, and Jacob Vigdor examined the relationship between an assessment of teacher effectiveness and how students are matched to teachers, using 3842 grade 5 teachers in 1160 elementary schools in North Carolina in 2000–2001.[4] Using scores on the two PRAXIS tests these teachers had taken for elementary licensure (PRAXIS 0011 and PRAXIS 0012) and on the state's student tests in mathematics and reading, the study found that the positive correlations between teacher qualifications (as measured by experience and licensure test scores) and student achievement were explained largely by the match between students and teachers across schools. Experience was more important than licensure test score only for socioeconomically higher and more able students in mathematics.

Other kinds of relationships with teacher quality have been examined. For example, in a 1998 report for the Pennsylvania State Board of Education, Robert Strauss examined the relationship between hiring decisions and teacher test scores.[5] According to his report, Pennsylvania awards 20,000 new elementary teaching licenses each year while less than 2,000 new elementary teachers are hired in the state annually; that is, its training institutions prepare far more elementary teachers than the state needs. The pass scores on the ETS tests it uses, set by panels of Pennsylvania teachers, are very low: about 90 percent of test takers pass the tests after answering from 25 percent to 60 percent of the questions correctly. (In comparison, Strauss noted, 48 percent annually pass Pennsylvania's law boards, and only 18 percent its CPA exams.) Graduates from some teacher training institutions answer only from 20 to 40 percent of the questions, while graduates from others correctly answer from 50 to 75 percent. Strauss found no statistically significant relationship between hiring decisions and teacher test scores; that is, local schools do not necessarily hire the most academically qualified teachers. However, "where districts utilize more professional personnel procedures in their recruitment of teachers, student achievement is generally higher. Where more emphasis is given to matters of residency and non-academic matters, student achievement is lower."

In a Working Paper issued in 2003 by the National Bureau of Economic Research (later published in 2004), Joshua Angrist and Jonathan Guryan addressed the question of whether teacher testing raises teacher quality.[6] Using Schools and Staffing Survey data to estimate the effect of teacher tests on teacher wages and on teacher quality as measured by educational background, they found that teacher testing increased teacher wages but with no corresponding increase in quality.

In a 2006 study, Thomas Kane, Jonah Rockoff, and Douglas Staiger examined the relationship between teachers' certification status and student achievement.[7] Their study consisted of 10,000 "certified," "uncertified," and "alternatively certified" teachers of reading and mathematics in grades 4 to 8, and their students' scores on state tests in mathematics and reading in New York City's schools over a six-year period. The researchers found that teachers from traditional training programs were generally no more or no less effective than teachers from alternative (or no) programs (including a large number from Teach for America). More variation in effectiveness could be found within each status group than among them. The study could not address the usefulness of licensure tests in screening teaching candidates for their academic competence since to teach, most teachers in the study had to pass New York State's tests, regardless of entry route.

WHAT STUDIES OF PREDICTIVE VALIDITY TELL US

No matter what the researchers found about the predictive value of teacher licensure tests in these studies, we can actually learn extremely little from them for two reasons. First, we do not know what most licensure tests of subject area knowledge assess and, therefore, what passing them means. While the scores on the licensure tests taken by teachers in North Carolina and Pennsylvania were predictive of teacher effectiveness, and in Tennessee an academically stronger test predicted more effective teachers than did a weaker test, none of these studies examined what these tests measure in reading or mathematics.

Nor do we know what student achievement on the state mathematics tests in Tennessee, North Carolina, and Pennsylvania means since none of the studies provided information on the content of the state's student tests. These tests may not indicate a very high level of mathematics achievement if the distribution of NAEP state test results is used as the yardstick. While Pennsylvania's rating was about midway in rank order, North Carolina and Tennessee received two of the four lowest ratings in a study comparing the difference between the percentage of a state's students who scored at the proficiency level on the 2003 NAEP tests and the percentage of students who scored at the proficiency level on the state's own tests.[8] In other words, there is a huge difference between the percentage of students judged by Tennessee and North Carolina tests as proficient in reading and math and the percentage of students judged by NAEP tests as proficient in reading and math. These states had much higher percentages of "proficient" students on their own tests than on the NAEP tests (e.g., Tennessee's reading test found 87 percent of its eighth graders "proficient," while NAEP's grade 8 test found only 27 percent "proficient"). The problem could be the pass score a state uses for its student tests or weak test items.

Nevertheless, there is continued expectation of a meaningful relationship between teacher licensure test scores and student achievement. For example, the authors of a chapter in the *Handbook on the Assessment of Teachers,* after providing a wealth of information on the history of teacher assessment, efforts to measure teachers' knowledge in mathematics, methods for measuring professional mathematical knowledge, and contemporary approaches to testing teachers for licensure, express their belief that these tests should have predictive validity for teachers' classrooms.[9] It is not clear why they fail to note that test developers have consistently pointed out that these tests are not and never were constructed to predict teacher effectiveness. Even today, experts on the construction of teacher licensure tests, that is, people with experience reviewing the specifications and procedures for their development and validation, see them useful only for distinguishing between candidates with and without minimum levels of knowledge necessary for an entry-level teaching position.[10] Subject area tests are constructed to discriminate between those test takers who are and are not "just acceptably qualified individuals" (i.e., *just* at the level of subject matter knowledge required for entry-level teaching in the field), and that is all. Raw scores on a licensure test might have a loose relationship with student achievement, but those who don't pass a licensure test based on pass/fail don't get a license to teach.

STUDIES OF THE CONSTRUCT OR CONTENT VALIDITY OF TEACHER TESTS

What has been needed from the inception of teacher testing are studies of their construct validity—that is, do they measure what they should measure or claim to measure. That is why a National Research Council volume titled *Testing Teacher Candidates: The Role of Licensure Tests in Improving Teacher Quality* is mystifying.[11] Although this volume was expressly concerned with the general content validity of teacher tests and their technical, or psychometric, qualities, its nine chapters provide no information on the quality of the content of any licensure test, the difficulty level of the items on any test, and the distribution of the content covered on any test. Nor do its editors explain why they did not address these topics or the level of the pass scores on teacher tests. The holes in this volume are especially puzzling because one of the few studies of the content of teacher tests, Mitchell and Barth's study, had been published by Education Trust in 1999.

Mitchell and Barth examined both teacher skills tests and subject area licensure tests, chiefly in English and mathematics.[12] Based on the judgment of the academic experts they used in the study, they concluded that current teacher skills tests are for the most part academically weak. Two-thirds of the mathematics items on PRAXIS I, a test of teachers' basic skills, were judged to be at the middle school level, with fewer items on algebra and geometry than on the 1996 grade 8 NAEP mathematics test. They praised the sample items on NES's skills test for prospective teachers and administrators in Massachusetts, which they considered more complex and demanding than any of the others they looked at. They judged the test to have a level of difficulty comparable to a college examination. Nevertheless, they did not judge even one of the skills tests they examined as close to the level of a graduating college senior. Overall, they judged the tests of teachers' skills at the "8th to 10th (sometimes 7th) grade level."

They judged the overall content of the subject tests they examined about the same as in "high-level high school courses," with a "few under-used exceptions." They found most mathematics licensure tests dominated by "simple recall" in multiple-choice items. They judged secondary mathematics tests to be at the 10th to 11th grade level. They judged those required for elementary licensure as a whole "at about the tenth grade level." According to their analysis, licensing tests fail to ask for a deep knowledge of the key concepts connected to the field of the license.

Mitchell and Barth viewed the system as "designed to prevent false negative judgments (about either candidates or the institutions that produce them)." "Underlying the whole process," they believe, "is the assumption that teachers only need to know the content that is expected of their students, and maybe just a little bit more." This assumption is made more explicit by the low pass scores states tend to set, such that passing a licensing exam "can mean nothing more than a high school diploma." They urged a loosening of the "stranglehold that litigation and psychometrics have on developing licensing examinations" so that they can become "instruments that signify high professional standards."

In another study of test content, a 2006 report for the National Council for Accreditation of Teacher Education (NCATE), Diana Rigden examined five tests provided by ETS for licensing elementary teachers, as well as the information NES provided on the reading tests it had developed for three states.[13] She wanted to see if these eight tests address the knowledge base for effective reading instruction. Rigden found that only one of the ETS tests (PRAXIS 0201), a reading rest required only in Tennessee (and for which test takers get credit simply by taking it), and the three NES tests have items that address the five components of scientifically based reading instruction. She observed that PRAXIS 0011, a multiple-choice test commonly used for elementary licensure in ETS states, "is not a good measure of a teacher candidate's knowledge of the five components of effective reading instruction." It should be noted that 35 percent of its test items address reading instruction.

In a study of the information that testing companies provide about their tests for prospective elementary teachers, Sandra Stotsky (2006) concluded that most of these tests do not assess adequately (if at all) research-supported knowledge of reading instruction.[14] Stotsky also examined the information on a relatively new set of PRAXIS tests called Principles of Learning and Teaching. This set of tests (one for each of four different educational levels) is designed to assess "what a beginning teacher should know about teaching and learning." According to the ETS website, 18 states require these tests in addition to a subject test. To judge by sample constructed-response and multiple-choice questions as well as the sample responses and question answers for these tests, this set of tests strongly promotes constructivist pedagogies and discredits alternative pedagogies.

WHAT STUDIES OF CONSTRUCT OR CONTENT VALIDITY TELL US

First, studies of construct or content validity implicitly raise questions about the worth of a teacher test. For example, both PRAXIS 0011 and PRAXIS 0012, the licensure tests used in Goldhaber's 2006 study, are described as measuring the knowledge and skills needed for teaching reading, mathematics, and other subjects in the elementary grades. Higher quintile status on these two tests predicted higher student achievement in reading and math in grades 4 and 6 on state tests. Yet, Rigden's 2006 analysis of the content of PRAXIS 0011 found few or no questions on research-based reading instruction in its reading section (which constitutes 35 percent of the test; mathematics test items are 20 percent of the test). What does one make of this anomaly? Is the research on reading instruction seriously flawed? Are the student tests seriously flawed as measures of reading achievement? Do the test items assess a candidate's ability to parrot a pedagogical party line in reading?

Perhaps other explanations are possible for this puzzling finding (a relationship between higher student achievement and higher scores on licensure tests that assess non-research-supported reading instructional knowledge). Clotfelter, Ladd, and Vigdor's study suggests that the relationship between higher quintile status on these two licensure tests and higher student achievement in *mathematics* in North Carolina might reflect a third factor—the higher socioeconomic status of the students in the classrooms of teachers with higher test scores. However, it may not be wise for researchers to make any claims when using student tests with unexamined content and when the licensure test in question may not be worth using to license elementary teachers.

Second, there are large differences across tests that purport to measure the same thing or some of the same things. For example, one can conclude from table 9.1, based on my 2009 study of online descriptions of tests for prospective special education teachers addressing mathematics content and three research-supported components of reading instructional knowledge, that in only seven states do prospective teachers seem to be assessed sufficiently on their knowledge of the development of phonemic awareness, phonics, and vocabulary.[15] One may also conclude that they are minimally assessed on their mathematical knowledge, regardless of the state they seek licensure in, if there is no separate test of mathematics.

Table 9.1. Estimated Percentage of Test Addressing Three Components of Reading Pedagogical Knowledge (Vocabulary, Phonemic Awareness, and Phonics) and Mathematics Content

Licensure Tests Assessing Reading Pedagogical Knowledge for Prospective Elementary and Sometimes Other Teachers*	Percent in Three Areas of Reading	Percent of Mathematics Content
PRAXIS 0011 (*Elementary Education: Curriculum, Instruction, and Assessment*), ETS (17 states)	7%	22%
PRAXIS 0012 (*Elementary Education: Content Area Exercises*), ETS (7 states)	1%	25%
PRAXIS 0014 (*Elementary Education: Content Knowledge*), ETS (22 states)	3%	25%
PRAXIS 0201 (*Reading across the Curriculum: Elementary*), ETS (1 state)	39%	0%
Multiple Subjects Exam (*for Elementary Education*), ABCTE**	9–10%	27%
Reading Endorsement for K–6, ABCTE	38%	0%
California RICA, NES** (1 state)	45–50%	0%

Licensure Tests Assessing Reading Pedagogical Knowledge for Prospective Elementary and Sometimes Other Teachers*	Percent in Three Areas of Reading	Percent of Mathematics Content
Connecticut (Foundations of Reading Test), ESP**** (1 state)	54%	0%
Illinois 110 (Elementary/Middle), NES (1 state)	5–6%	20%
Michigan 83 (Elementary Education), NES (1 state)	2%	20%
Massachusetts 90 (Foundations of Reading), NES*** (1 state)	54%	0%
Minnesota Elementary Education (Subtest I), ESP (1 state)	40%	0%
New York 02 (Multi-Subject Test: Grades Pre-K–9), NES (1 state)	12%	18%
Oklahoma 50 (Elementary Education Subtest I), NES (1 state)	25%	0%
Virginia VRA, NES *** (1 state)	25%	0%
Licensure Tests for Prospective Special Education Teachers		
PRAXIS 0353 (Education of Exceptional Students: Core Content Knowledge), ETS	0%	0%
PRAXIS 0351 (Special Education: Knowledge-Based Core Principles), ETS	0%	0%
PRAXIS 0511 (Fundamental Subjects: Content Knowledge), ETS	1%	25%
Special Education (K–6), ABCTE	9%	0%
Illinois 155 (Learning Behavior Specialist I), NES	1%	1%
Michigan 63 (Learning Disabled), NES	4%	1%
New York 60 (Students with Disabilities, CST), NES	1%	1%

* The number of states requiring the test for prospective elementary teachers is in parentheses after its title.

** Required of both prospective elementary and special education teachers in the state.

*** Required of prospective elementary, early childhood, and special education teachers in the state.

**** Required of both prospective elementary and early childhood teachers in the state.

Without an examination of the test items on these tests, we cannot tell exactly how well they are assessed on these three aspects of beginning reading instruction or what mathematics knowledge they are being assessed on. But the overall percentages for these content areas indicate that those who are licensed by these tests may bring very different levels of academic competence to their teaching.

NOTES

1. J. Boot, *Student Achievement and* Passport to Teaching *Certification in Elementary Education* (Washington, DC: American Board for Certification of Teacher Excellence, 2006).

2. J. Boot, *Student Achievement and* Passport to Teaching *Certification in Mathematics* (Washington, DC: American Board for Certification of Teacher Excellence, 2007). http://www.abcte.org/files/math_2007_validity.pdf.

3. D. Goldhaber, *Everyone's Doing It, but What Does Teacher Testing Tell Us about Teacher Effectiveness?* (Seattle: University of Washington and the Urban Institute, 2006).

4. C. Clotfelter, H. Ladd, and J. Vigdor, *Teacher-Student Matching and the Assessment of Teacher Effectiveness*, Working Paper 11936 (Cambridge, MA: National Bureau of Economic Research, 2006). http://www.nber.org/papers/w11936.

5. R. Strauss, *Teacher Preparation and Selection in Pennsylvania*, Research Report to the Pennsylvania State Board of Education, 1998.

6. J. Angrist, and J. Guryan, *Does Teacher Testing Raise Teacher Quality: Evidence from State Certification Requirements*, Working Paper 9545 (Cambridge, MA: National Bureau of Economic Research, 2003).

7. T. Kane, J. Rockoff, and D. Staiger, *What Does Certification Tell Us about Teacher Effectiveness? Evidence from New York City* (Cambridge, MA: Harvard Graduate School of Education, 2006).

8. Paul Peterson and Rick Hess, "Johnny Can Read . . . in Some States," *Education Next*, 2005, 5(3), 52–53.

9. H. Hill, L. Sleep, J. Lewis, and D. Ball, "Assessing Teachers' Mathematical Knowledge: What Knowledge Matters and What Evidence Counts?," in *Second Handbook of Research on Mathematics Teaching and Learning*, ed. F. Lester (Charlotte, NC: Information Age Publishing, 2007), 111–55.

10. William Mehrens, Stephen Klein, and Robert Gabrys, *Report by the Technical Advisory Committee on the Massachusetts Tests for Educator Licensure*, submitted to the Massachusetts Department of Education and Commissioner of Education, January 14, 2002. http://archives.lib.state.ma.us/handle/2452/202377.

11. K. Mitchell, D. Robinson, B. Plake, and K. Knowles, *Testing Teacher Candidates: The Role of Licensure Tests in Improving Teacher Quality*, National Research Council (Washington, DC: National Academy Press, 2001).

12. Ruth Mitchell and Patte Barth, "Not Good Enough: A Content Analysis of Teacher Licensing Examinations. How Teacher Licensing Tests Fall Short," *Thinking K–16*, 1999, 3(1), 3–23.

13. Diana Rigden, *Report on Licensure Alignment with the Essential Components of Effective Reading Instruction*, report commissioned by the National Council for Accreditation of Teacher Education, 2006. http://edexcellence.net/commentary/education-gadfly-weekly/2006/september-14/report-on-licensure-alignment-with-the-essential-components-of-effective-reading-instruction.html.

14. Sandra Stotsky, "Why American Students Do Not Learn to Read Very Well: The Unintended Consequences of Title II and Teacher Testing," Third Education Group Review, 2006, 2(2), 1–37.

15. Sandra Stotsky, "Licensure Tests for Special Education Teachers: How Well They Assess Knowledge of Reading Instruction and Mathematics," *Journal of Learning Disabilities*, September/October 2009, 42(5), 464–74. http://ldx.sagepub.com/cgi/content/abstract/42/5/464.

10

DIFFICULTIES IN REQUIRING MORE DEMANDING SUBJECT AREA LICENSURE TESTS

Some policy makers propose national teacher tests as a way to solve the problem of test variability across states. A national test could legitimately (legally) be required of all those either completing a teacher preparation program subsidized by the federal government or seeking a teaching position in a school subsidized by the federal government. But national teacher tests are as unlikely as state tests to guarantee academic competence. National subject tests are likely to be as short as state tests are. And there is every reason to believe that government-sponsored teacher tests would be as vulnerable as state tests are to the demands of special interest groups or to the influence of the "language police" and other censors who lurk behind the scenes for every test constructed in this country today, including those by the National Assessment of Educational Progress. Who should shape their blueprints? Who should construct them? Who should establish their scoring procedures? Where should the cut scores be? And last but hardly least, would the public be able to monitor their development, contents, and scoring procedures? Indeed, the public might be as much in the dark about the influences on a national teacher test as they are about the influences on their state teacher tests. After describing some of the problems the states face in strengthening their teacher licensure tests academically, this chapter suggests where a guarantee of a prospective teacher's academic competence should come from.

ANOMALY OF TEACHER LICENSURE TESTS

The possibility of national teacher tests raises a question that has not surfaced in discussions of state licensure tests for teachers. These tests have a peculiar limitation that makes them very different from the national or state exams taken by graduates of our medical schools, nursing colleges, law schools, schools of architecture, and other professional schools. All candidates for admission to these and most other professions must take licensing tests (sometimes both a nationwide test and a state-specific test), whether they plan to work for the government, for private agencies, or for themselves.

In contrast, licensure tests for K–12 teachers are usually required only for those who teach in our public schools. Teachers in private schools in most states do not need to be licensed. Nor do teachers in many states' public charter schools, to make this exemption even more anomalous. Home-schooling parents do not need to be licensed, either. How would a national policy handle these exemptions when state policies themselves do not make sense?

We also need to consider how these exemptions may contribute to the relatively low quality of teacher licensure tests. It is not well-known that teacher licensure tests for a particular state must be peer-reviewed chiefly by public school teachers in that state holding a license in the subject of the test under review. The peers may not necessarily be the academically strongest teachers of that subject. For example, many of the academically strongest teachers who teach debating, rhetoric, and public speaking in Massachusetts teach at independent Catholic high schools, I was told. Yet, because they typically don't hold a teaching license they could not serve on review or "standard-setting" committees for licensure tests in Speech in the Bay State.

CLAIMS ABOUT THE SUPPLY AND ACADEMIC QUALITY OF PROSPECTIVE TEACHERS

Many economists view licensure tests as "obstacles" or "barriers" to teaching and call for their removal. However, in Massachusetts, there is no evidence that they have served as obstacles or barriers. To the contrary. In 2001, just a few years after teacher testing began, about 60

percent of the test takers passed the two tests required for initial licensing—the state's skills test for prospective teachers and administrators
and the test of subject area knowledge. In 1998, the year the tests
began, about 60 percent failed both tests.

Moreover, there was an immediate increase in the mean pass rates
for each quartile of the state's 58 institutions with approved teacher-
licensure programs, a ranking system required for Title II reports beginning with the 1999–2000 cohort of prospective teachers. For example, the mean pass rate for the lowest quartile in academic content was
64.8 for the 1999–2000 cohort and 68.2 for the 2001–2002 cohort; the
mean pass rate for the highest quartile in academic content was 96.1 for
the 1999–2000 cohort and 99.9 for the 2001–2002 cohort.

Nor has the overall number of first-time, subject area test takers
declined. Indeed, the overall number of test takers has remained re-
markably steady from year to year. Comparing the number of first-time
test takers at the March test administrations from 2005 to 2012, we find
that in March 2005, there were 4612 first-time subject area test takers;
in March 2006, 4958; in March 2007, 4712; in March 2008, 4383; in
March 2009, 5265; in March 2010, 5568; in March 2011, 5373; and in
March 2012, 4966.[1] However, these numbers are much higher than the
number of first-time subject area test takers at test administrations before test takers had to take the new or revised licensing tests (a little
over 3000 first-time test takers at the February 2002 test administration, and many fewer in earlier years).

The pass rate was also fairly steady for the total number of first-time
subject area test takers, hovering between 60 percent and 70 percent
across these years. So, the revised tests are harder, the numbers of first-
time test takers taking them are much higher, but the percentage passing is about the same. This suggests that the pass scores may have been
lowered (by the "standard-setting" peer review committee or the commissioner of education) for the revised tests—before scaling (which
makes all scores comparable across tests and test years). Thus, even if
prospective teachers are passing with a possibly lower raw score, they
are taking a more difficult licensing test to do so. A commissioner of
education can always recommend to the state board of education that it
raise the pass scores (on tests worth taking), but that is a political decision on how many should be allowed to pass and enter a profession.

It should be noted that many teacher training programs in the state require a passing grade on the subject area test *before* a prospective teacher is allowed to do practice teaching. But there are no public records showing when each of the many teacher preparation programs in the state initiated this practice. This practice might possibly have spurred aspiring teachers to try to do well on their subject area tests if they wanted to do their student teaching in the following fall of the calendar year in which they took the March test. The same percentages would pass the licensing tests (over time), they might be told, but the tests would be harder.

At the same time, the Massachusetts teacher tests seem to have eliminated a large number of academically unqualified candidates. Varying percentages of prospective teachers across the different subject areas have not passed the subject area test required for their license the first time they took their tests. At the March 2012 test administration, for example, for first-time test takers, only 47 percent in Earth Science passed; in Chemistry, only 49 percent; in General Science, 86 percent; in English, 84 percent; and in Mathematics, 75 percent. Keep in mind that the raw numbers are not large in many fields, especially in the sciences, and while those who fail a licensing test on the first try can retake the test, the available statistics do not indicate how many times they retake the test or when they pass, if they do. Some of those who eventually pass have taken the test more than once, a few more than six or seven times. However, the number and percentage of those who pass after failing the first time is consistently small.

Education faculty at Massachusetts institutions of higher education have long criticized the Massachusetts teacher tests on psychometric grounds, despite a positive technical review in 2002 by nationally prominent experts on large-scale assessment and licensing procedures. But the criticism may be motivated by the impression that the Massachusetts tests are generally harder than most PRAXIS tests, as Mitchell and Barth suggested in their 1999 article in Education Trust's quarterly journal.[2]

Nevertheless, so far as can be determined from the few studies that have examined the content of licensure tests or from anecdotal reports by those who managed to take a licensure test, most subject area tests in this country, regardless of test developer, are still not equivalent in difficulty to department-based examinations for undergraduates completing a major in a particular discipline. Most skills tests are at the middle school to lower high school level. So it is difficult to see teacher licensing tests, either the skills tests or the subject area tests, as obstacles or barriers for those who want to become K–12 teachers, given that they must be college graduates.

MEASURE OF VALUE-ADDED, NOT DISCIPLINARY, KNOWLEDGE: WHICH IS PREFERABLE?

Many economists interested in free market theories have advocated eliminating licensure tests for teachers on the grounds that they pose unnecessary barriers for people who might become good teachers and that the "market" should decide. Such a position seems to presume that their training programs would weed out people who would become poor teachers, although there is no evidence to suggest that teacher training programs have done or could do this on a meaningful scale. Indeed, the attention being paid to ways to identify "ineffective" teachers and the intention of Race to the Top grants to hold teachers accountable for student scores on Common Core–based tests suggest they populate our public schools in large numbers.

To identify such teachers statistically, many economists and others have promoted "value-added" methodologies. These are objective measures of teachers' effectiveness based on their student scores over a period of several years on presumably valid and reliable tests. Such measures could be used to dismiss poor teachers as well as show long-term benefits for students having a teacher (or a series of teachers) deemed effective. An example of such a study was published in a 2014 issue of the prestigious *American Economic Review*.[3] It found that over a lifetime of projected earnings, a student of such a teacher might earn about $15,000 more than a student of another teacher would.

The limitations of value-added methodologies are the subject of professional debate today (for example, a 2014 review by Matthew Di Carlo in a Shanker Blog[4]). Whether parents would want school systems to hire new teachers who had passed a test showing a high degree of academic knowledge in the subject to be taught, or to rely on recommendations from a teacher training program and wait for the results of statistical tests of effectiveness after the new teacher has taught for several years, is a question that needs discussion. While academically knowledgeable teachers might not necessarily be effective teachers, it is hard to imagine an effective teacher who is not academically knowledgeable.

There is no reason why both kinds of measures could not be used. Common sense alone would suggest that school systems hire academically knowledgeable teachers to begin with. In other words, passing a subject area licensing test would be necessary but not sufficient.

PROCEDURAL OBSTACLES

There are at least five procedural reasons why it will not be easy to develop more academically rigorous teacher tests tailored to demanding K–12 academic standards.

1. *Opposition by many members of such a "standard-setting" committee to a more demanding licensure test in their area.* It is not illogical for both education school faculty and arts and sciences faculty on a committee charged with raising the pass score on a subject area licensure test to predict that if fewer test takers pass a more demanding test, then the number of undergraduate students seeking admission to the education school or seeking to major in that area may decline. Thus, they may not raise the pass score if left to their own self-interest. So, too, may the K–12 teachers on the committee not raise the pass score. Is it in their interest to have more academically competent colleagues? How many of them already believe that tests of academic achievement are detrimental to efforts to get more minority students into teaching (with all that implies about their view of minority students)? How many of them already believe that pedagogical knowledge is much more important than academic knowledge despite the research finding on the characteristics of an effective teacher?

2. *Misuse by many education schools of the subject area licensure test by requiring it to be passed before allowing undergraduates to do student teaching.* A more demanding test might mean fewer prospective teachers completing a preparation program after tak-

ing the coursework leading to student teaching. This misuse of the subject area licensure test may already affect the quality of the intellectual experience these undergraduates should obtain from their major. If they pass the subject area test for their license at the end of their junior year or by the beginning of their senior year, they are unlikely to take any more upper-level courses in their major, or in the arts and sciences altogether, if they have already fulfilled the requisite number of credit hours for the major or in the arts and sciences.

3. *Few test preparation workshops offered by education schools for the subject area test.* This is not surprising since education schools are not responsible for the content taught in the arts and sciences. But the more basic problem is the low level of involvement by arts and sciences faculty in developing, reviewing, and setting a standard for the licensure test in their own discipline, in the construction (with colleagues in the education school) of pedagogical courses for their discipline, and in the supervision of student teaching in classes in their discipline.

4. *The existence of undergraduate licensure programs.* Why is a subject test needed at all if the prospective candidate has in fact completed an appropriate major for the license sought and in an accredited college or university? The fact that subject area tests are required not just of prospective generalist teachers (e.g., elementary or early childhood teachers), but also of prospective subject teachers who tend to have completed a relevant major or strong minor, suggests that legislators do not trust the undergraduate college's graduation standards or the faculty's judgment about the courses it has approved for the major. Why require stronger subject area licensure tests unless one does not trust the arts and sciences faculty?

5. *Misuse of a subject area test for admission to a postbaccalaureate program in teacher preparation.* A more demanding test would reduce the number of those seeking admission to a program without an appropriate major or minor in the subject. At present, the misuse of a subject area test for admission to a postbaccalaureate program in teacher preparation baldly implies that undergraduate coursework in that subject is not necessary for a future teacher of that subject. All that matters is being able to pass the test.

Does it make sense professionally to imply that all that matters academically is passing a subject area licensure test, not also having taken demanding coursework in the subject? Should a subject area test for licensure be divorced from the academic course of studies it is in theory supposed to culminate?

The opposition that could arise if a legislature required more demanding subject area licensure tests raises a final question. Is a test of academic content (never mind a test of basic reading and writing skills) an appropriate licensure test for teachers? Or should a test of the quality of an academic course of studies precede the licensing test and be a college or university responsibility? This is not an argument against a licensing test of academic competence for a future teacher of a subject here. This is a question only about whether such a test should also be constructed and given by the college or university faculty. The purpose for such a test would be to determine if an undergraduate has satisfactorily completed in-depth study of a subject (i.e., for a major or concentration) as part of fulfilling graduation requirements for a bachelor's degree. Its results would contribute to the acceptance or rejection of a prospective teacher in a postbaccalaureate teacher licensure program. Then, a test of subject area knowledge could be developed by the state and used, appropriately, at the completion of a teacher preparation program for the purpose of licensure (and entry into a profession).

NOTES

1. "Massachusetts Tests for Educator Licensure (MTEL): Number of Examinees and Percent of Examinees Passing Each Test by Examinee Category," Massachusetts Department of Elementary and Secondary Education, 2014. http://www.doe.mass.edu/mtel/results/2013–1125.html.

2. Ruth Mitchell and Patte Barth, "Not Good Enough: A Content Analysis of Teacher Licensing Examinations. How Teacher Licensing Tests Fall Short," *Thinking K–16*, 1999, 3(1), 3–23.

3. Raj Chetty, John N. Friedman, and Jonah E. Rockoff, "Measuring the Impacts of Teachers II: Teacher Value-Added and Student Outcomes in Adulthood," *American Economic Review*, 2014, 104(9): 2633–79. http://dx.doi.org/10.1257/aer.104.9.2633.

4. Matthew Di Carlo, "A Quick Look at the ASA Statement on Value-Added," August 26, 2014, Shanker Blog. http://shankerblog.org/?p=10371.

11

WHAT STATE LEGISLATORS PROBABLY SHOULDN'T DO

One purpose for teacher licensure tests was—and remains—to upgrade teacher preparation programs. That was the fond hope behind a provision in Title II of the 1998 reauthorization of the Higher Education Act (HEA) requiring each state to report annually the pass rates on tests of its own choosing for prospective teachers graduating from its teacher training institutions. Lawmakers believed that negative publicity about low pass rates would encourage low-performing teacher training programs to strengthen their programs.

This utopian expectation might have borne some fruit if even a few training programs ended up with low pass rates followed by negative publicity. But as it turned out, *mirabile dictu*, not one training program in the country ended up with a low pass rate. This chapter will explain why. But first we look at what state legislators shouldn't do.

FAIL TO ASK FOR STRONGER QUALITY CONTROLS

Among many other agencies, the U.S. Department of Education (USDE) is rightfully not satisfied with the quality of this country's teaching force. To judge by the criteria in its 2010 Race to the Top (RTTT) application material, we don't have the kind of teachers we need, at least enough of them and in the right places. However, the USDE seems to have a zero-sum game in mind with respect to "effective teachers." It seeks to distribute equitably the "effective" teachers a state may already have, instead of trying to ensure a potentially effective teacher for everyone. Only 14 points at the most could be awarded for a state's plan to strengthen its teacher preparation programs. But up to 21 points could be awarded for "providing high-quality pathways for aspiring teachers and principals." Stunningly, this criterion implied that existing preparation programs are not high-quality pathways for aspiring teachers.

Worse yet, no points were explicitly set forth for detailed plans to recruit academically competent individuals for a teaching career (which is not the same thing as providing high-quality pathways for those who want to become teachers) or for ensuring that those who are given a license to teach a subject are academically qualified to teach it. This enormous hole ignores what high-quality research tells us—that the chief characteristic of an effective teacher is knowledge of the subject he or she teaches—a finding highlighted in a task group report on teachers and teacher education to the National Mathematics Advisory Panel in March 2008.[1] There is no consistent evidence for any other characteristic despite efforts of educational researchers to find one.

In addition, the USDE missed the opportunity to call attention to the quality controls in place in other countries that ensure the academic competence of those allowed to become teachers. These quality controls not only assure parents that their children's teachers are academically qualified but also dramatically reduce the need for seemingly massive and endless amounts of professional development—a distinctly American phenomenon. No other country would spend what we lavish on professional development for already licensed teachers, especially when so much of it is remedial in nature and there is so little evidence of its effectiveness.

It is a peculiarly American belief that one relatively short and easy subject area test constructed for licensing purposes (not as an achievement test) serves as the best way to determine the adequacy of a prospective teacher's academic background in a core subject. The typical teacher test of academic content requires little more than three hours of the test taker's time, if that, and involves no more than 100 to 125 test items, mostly multiple choice in nature. Few if any other countries subscribe to such minimalist standards for assessing the academic preparation of their future teachers, especially those who teach core subjects at the secondary level.

LEAVE ACADEMIC ADMISSION STANDARDS ALONE

The academic caliber of female teachers, who continue to comprise the bulk of the elementary school teaching force, is no longer as strong as it once was. Several reports have been issued in the past decade alone (e.g., a McKinsey report in 2010[2]) noting that this country's teaching force comes from the bottom third of its college cohort. Careful studies have clearly documented the decline in the academic competence of our teaching force in the past 50 years, especially the study by economists Caroline Hoxby and Andrew Leigh, 2005.[3] I describe here the most recent one, a study by Marigee Bacolod.

A labor economist at the University of California in Irvine at the time her research was published in 2007, Marigee Bacolod brought together several sources of information to document a change in the composition of women who chose to teach between 1960 and 1990.[4] Her information came mainly from standardized test scores and undergraduate institution selectivity. Bacolod found that teacher performance on standardized exams had declined—markedly so among women—relative to previous cohorts of teachers and to professionals in their own cohort. Her data clearly suggested that "as outside opportunities improved for women and blacks in the recent decades, fewer [high-achieving women] chose to teach, and those who did teach tended to be less skilled." All the reasons for the decline are not clear, although Hoxby and Leigh's study suggested that the wages paid teachers once women were encouraged to enter other professions was a major reason for the decline. Whatever the reasons, there is no reason for not addressing it.

RELY ON ACCREDITATION

In his 2006 report, *Educating School Teachers,* Arthur Levine, former president of Teachers College, Columbia University, recommended closing down the vast bulk of the 1200 education schools in this country on the grounds that they have incoherent curricula as well as excessively low admission standards.[5] He also concluded that accreditation has been a useless instrument for upgrading academic requirements for teacher preparation programs. He found no relationship between accreditation and teacher quality or student achievement.

Many schools of education have been accredited in recent decades by two private agencies—the National Council for Accreditation of Teacher Education (NCATE) and the Teacher Education Accreditation Council (TEAC). Many had also been influenced by the standards or principles recommended by the Interstate New Teacher Assessment and Support Consortium (INTASC).

One reason that accreditation failed to influence the academic competence of new teachers is its conflation of pedagogical content knowledge (the professional skills and knowledge needed to teach a particular subject at a particular educational level to particular kinds of children) with the subject area knowledge acquired by those interested in a discipline, whether or not they choose to become teachers of that discipline in K–12. The contributions of courses in the arts and sciences and courses in schools of education are simply merged for the purpose of evaluating teacher preparation programs.

The blurring of the distinctive contribution of pedagogical and academic coursework to teacher quality can be seen in the standards or principles for accrediting teacher preparation programs to be used by the Council for the Accreditation of Education Preparation (CAEP), the newly formed merger of NCATE and TEAC. The first of four broad standards for accreditation, approved in August 2013, is titled "Standard 1: Content and Pedagogical Knowledge." It is explained as follows: "The provider [of the teacher preparation program] ensures that candidates develop a deep understanding of the critical concepts and principles of their discipline and, by completion, are able to use discipline-specific practices flexibly to advance the learning of all students toward attainment of college- and career-readiness standards."[6]

In other words, there is no separate accreditation standard on whether prospective teachers have an adequate grasp of the content of what they will teach before they complete a training program. CAEP's accreditation standard seems to suggest a merger of two different kinds of assessments, leaving it unclear whether the candidate for a teaching license in a subject area has an adequate grasp of the subject area independent of students' difficulties with the subject, or cannot adequately teach students who have failed to learn the topic for reasons that have little or nothing to do with the teacher's knowledge of the subject.

Such a confused accreditation standard betrays a misconception of what should be assessed before a would-be teacher's admission to a training program and by whom. Then, the question of whether the prospective teacher knows how to teach a particular subject is what preparation programs assess in student teaching and with discipline-based supervisors, as well as education faculty jointly making the assessment.

REQUIRE STATES TO REPORT PASS RATES ANNUALLY

During the 2000s, comprehensive reports were issued by national panels of distinguished scholars and researchers on the most effective methods/coursework for teaching reading and mathematics based on evidence from only high-quality research. There is no evidence of a positive response to these reports by our education schools. Programs for prospective elementary teachers are the best case to examine because they have long needed more academic strengthening than programs for prospective secondary teachers (who tend to have majored in what they aim to teach).

In April 2000, the National Reading Panel (NRP) issued its report, *Teaching Children to Read*, indicating the major elements in effective, beginning reading instruction.[7] Based on an analysis of the high-quality studies available, this report highlighted the importance of phonemic awareness, knowledge of sound/letter relationships, fluency, vocabulary knowledge, and general comprehension of written language in the development of reading skills. As the report indicated, most children must receive systematic instruction in phonemic awareness for distinguishing the sounds in words, and in phonics for identifying printed words. The report also noted that they must also read aloud regularly to demonstrate fluency, practice enough to acquire decoding skills to the point of automaticity, and receive systematic instruction through the grades to develop their knowledge of word meanings.

Despite the fact that the crucial role of these five strategies for teaching beginning reading had been established by a careful review of the research and reported in a publication prepared by nationally recognized experts, two studies completed well after 2000 (one in 2004, the other in 2006) found few schools of education teaching prospective teachers about these five strategies or the research base for them in reading methods courses.[8]

What could be found, of course, was criticism of the NRP report and the two studies, both of which had based their conclusions on an examination of the syllabi the researchers could locate for reading methods courses in education schools. One complaint was that not all syllabi used in reading methods courses in education schools had been examined. Another criticism was that the sample of syllabi used was not a truly random sample. A few reading educators criticized the composition of the National Reading Panel itself.

Nevertheless, no one argued that the five strategies that the 2000 NRP report highlighted for their effectiveness did not warrant study in reading methods coursework. Nor, despite their complaints about the methodology of the two studies or the composition of the NRP panel, did the critics in our education schools present evidence using a methodology of their own choice that these strategies or the research evidence supporting them were in fact being studied in coursework for prospective teachers. A similar scenario took place with respect to mathematics coursework for prospective elementary teachers.

The National Mathematics Advisory Panel (NMAP) issued its report in March 2008, indicating what the research evidence suggests will increase mathematics achievement in preschool, elementary school, and middle school.[9] The report also identified 27 major topics of school algebra and set forth the crucial mathematical concepts and skills in pre-K–7, whose mastery could lead to success in Algebra I. These critical concepts and skills were organized in three categories described below: Fluency with Whole Numbers, Fluency with Fractions, and Particular Aspects of Geometry and Measurement.

Fluency with Whole Numbers includes understanding of place value; fluency in composing and decomposing whole numbers; understanding of the meaning of the basic operations of addition, subtraction, multiplication, and division; automatic recall of number facts; fluency with the standard algorithms for addition, subtraction, multiplication, and division; and knowledge of how to apply these operations to problem solving.

Fluency with Fractions includes a thorough understanding of positive and negative fractions as well as the ability to locate fractions on the number line; to represent and compare fractions, decimals, and related percents; and to estimate their size. Students also need to know that sums, differences, products, and quotients (with non-zero denominators) of fractions are fractions; why and how (finite) decimal numbers are fractions; and the meaning of percentages.

Particular Aspects of Geometry and Measurement includes experience with similar triangles because sound treatments of the slope of a straight line and of linear functions depend logically on the properties of similar triangles.

For instructional practices, the NMAP report identified the following teaching strategies as supported by high-quality research:

1. Explicit and systematic instruction for students with learning problems.
2. Formative assessment, especially at the elementary level.
3. Small group work and the use of "real-world" problems, but only under very specific conditions, at certain grade levels, and chiefly for developing computational skills.

In addition, the NMAP report found no research showing that teacher-directed learning prevents students from understanding mathematics. It also found that calculator use does not promote conceptual development, calculation skills, or problem solving.

The most important point the NMAP report made was a common sense one: It reaffirmed a teacher's knowledge of mathematics as the only identifiable characteristic of an effective mathematics teacher. Yet, the response of mathematics educators was to criticize the NMAP report on the grounds that it used only evidence from high-quality research to make its points about the pedagogy to teach prospective elementary teachers of mathematics. Like educators critical of the NRP report, mathematics educators, too, did not provide any evidence from studies of their own choosing that education school–based teacher preparation programs were providing the kind of mathematics coursework these prospective teachers need.

What they need was spelled out by the National Council on Teacher Quality in a study on the preparation of elementary teachers in mathematics in 77 institutions in 49 states.[10] It found only ten of these institutions providing adequate mathematics coursework for these aspiring teachers. How did it arrive at this finding? This 2008 study examined the time spent on the four areas of mathematics that an elementary teacher needs to understand: (1) numbers and operations, (2) algebra, (3) geometry and measurement, and (4) data analysis and probability. Of these four areas, the study found algebra instruction the weakest, with over half of all schools (52 percent) devoting less than 15 percent of class time to algebra, with another third effectively *ignoring it entirely*, devoting less than 5 percent of class time to that area. According to the mathematics advisory group for this study, algebra should comprise roughly 25 percent of the preparation in mathematics for elementary teachers because they need to understand it as the generalization of the arithmetic they address and its connection to many of the properties, relationships, rules, and models that elementary students study.

To judge by these studies on reading methods courses and mathematics coursework in elementary preparation programs, it appears that the 1998 reauthorization of the HEA did little if anything to upgrade the quality of our teacher education programs. Despite the fact that prospective teachers were on average less academically competent after 1990 than in 1960, teacher preparation programs were nevertheless reporting almost 100 percent pass rates on the licensure tests all aspiring teachers were required to pass after 1998. How was this possible? Here are some of the reasons.

1. In some institutions of higher education, the definition of "program completer" (a student in a teacher preparation program) was someone who passed the licensure tests required for the program. By definition, the program had a 100 percent pass rate.

2. In some institutions of higher education, admission to a graduate program for teacher preparation (an M.Ed. program) was contingent upon passing the licensure tests required for the program. (Remember, the law did not specify when the licensure tests could or should be given.) Prospective teachers would have to take and pass the teacher skills test and subject knowledge test

before admission to a postbaccalaureate program in teacher preparation. Therefore the program had a 100 percent pass rate.
3. Most licensure tests have such low pass scores that almost all
those taking them pass. Pass scores are not set to protect children
in our public schools from academically incompetent teachers.
They are set at levels to protect teacher preparation institutions
in this country, most of which receive taxpayers' money directly
from state appropriations or indirectly from USDE grants.

NOTES

1. National Mathematics Advisory Panel, *Report of the Task Group on Teachers and Teacher Education*, chaired by Deborah Loewenberg Ball, 2008, 5-x. https://www2.ed.gov/about/bdscomm/list/mathpanel/report/teachers.pdf.

2. Byron Auguste, Paul Kihn, and Matt Miller, "Closing the Talent Gap: Attracting and Retaining Top Third Graduates to a Career in Teaching," McKinsey and Company, 2010. http://mckinseyonsociety.com/closing-the-talent-gap/.

3. Carolyn Hoxby and Andrew Leigh, "Wage Distortion: Why America's Top Female Graduates Aren't Teaching," *Education Next*, Spring 2005, 50–56. http://faculty.smu.edu/millimet/classes/eco4361/readings/hoxby%20leigh%202005.pdf.

4. Marigee Bacolod, "Do Alternative Opportunities Matter? The Role of Female Labor Markets in the Decline of Teacher Quality," *The Review of Economics and Statistics*, 2007, 89(4): 737–51.

5. Arthur Levine, *Educating School Teachers* (Washington, DC: Education School Projects, September 2006). http://www.edschools.org/pdf/educating_teachers_report.pdf.

6. *CAEP Accreditation Standards and Evidence: Aspirations for Educator Preparation*, June 11, 2013. http://edsource.org/wp-content/uploads/commrpt.pdf.

7. Report of the National Reading Panel. "Teaching Children to Read: An Evidence-Based Assessment of the Scientific Research Literature on Reading and Its Implications for Reading Instruction" (Washington, DC: National Institute of Child Health and Human Development, 2000). NIH Publication No. 00-4769.

8. David Steiner, with Susan Rozen, "Preparing Tomorrow's Teachers: An Analysis of Syllabi from a Sample of America's Schools of Education," in *A Qualified Teacher in Every Classroom? Appraising Old Answers and New*

Ideas, eds. F. Hess, A. Rotherham, and K. Walsh (Cambridge, MA: Harvard Education Press, 2004), 119–48; Kate Walsh, Deborah Glaser, and Danielle Dunne Wilcox, *What Education School's Aren't Teaching about Reading and What Elementary Teachers Aren't Learning* (Washington, DC: National Council on Teacher Quality, 2006).

    9. National Mathematics Advisory Panel, *Foundations for Success: The Final Report of the National Mathematics Advisory Panel* (Washington, DC: U.S. Department of Education, 2008).

    10. Julie Greenberg and Kate Walsh, *No Common Denominator: The Preparation of Elementary Teachers in Mathematics by America's Education Schools* (Washington, DC: National Council on Teacher Quality, 2008).

12

WHAT POLICY MAKERS AND STATE LEGISLATORS CAN DO

Most teacher licensing regulations and tests do not reflect academic experts' ideas about what the content of their disciplines in the school curriculum should be or what the academic background prospective teachers of that subject should bring to their first classrooms. Instead, they tend to reflect the ideas of a state's commissioner and department of education staff, many of whom are influenced by the education schools they attended, teacher unions, school administrators' needs, the interests of professional education organizations, and the pressure of political groups (especially think tanks, institutes, and policy-oriented organizations that claim expertise on educational matters).

The ideas of all these groups or individuals about what should be taught in teacher preparation programs and assessed in student teaching or on teacher licensing tests influence teachers' ability to construct and teach to a sound K–12 curriculum. These ideas may be quite different from what parents want and think their taxes are paying for or what academic or occupational experts know K–12 students need for entering a specific occupation or enrolling in a particular postsecondary academic or occupational program. These ideas are often contrary to what credible research evidence suggests.

This chapter suggests what policy makers and state legislators can do to academically strengthen our public schools and the teachers in them. The suggestions are based on the changes made to the Bay State's teacher licensing regulations and licensing tests, as well as on the evidence that shows how these changes overall may have contributed to the "Massachusetts education miracle."

STRENGTHEN THE LICENSING SYSTEM FOR CTE TEACHERS AT ALL LEVELS

The licensure system for "shop" teachers, whether in vocational/technical high schools or in programs in regular high schools, now referred to as Career and Technical Education (CTE), differs from the system for academic teachers and differs from state to state, just as it does for academic licensure, but for a different reason. Many CTE teachers have only a high school diploma and come from many years of work experience in industry or have been self-employed (e.g., as a carpenter or electrician). They are usually expected to complete a certain amount of pedagogical and sometimes other coursework for full licensure. However, their pedagogical coursework may not be related to the occupational skills they teach (as it must be in Massachusetts), and it is not clear whether they must have industry-recognized expertise in the occupational area they teach.

Only teachers in the five original vocational areas of business education, home economics, agriculture, instructional technology, and industrial arts/technology have usually completed a traditional, four-year, undergraduate education in their occupational area and thus receive an "academic" license. All others are part of a vocational licensure or "permit" system, although their pedagogical coursework and graduate degrees may be in traditional schools of education.

At the postsecondary level, teaching qualifications for CTE instructors tend to be minimal. Teachers in postsecondary technical schools may or may not have an occupational certificate (these teachers are generally not licensed by the state) and may have no more than a degree from a technical school in the occupational area they teach, if that—a stunning situation at a time when we expect a rapidly growing number of graduating high school students to enroll in a postsecondary program in these technical schools.

The situation is also disturbing because CTE high school programs tend to enroll a disproportionate share of the most difficult-to-educate students; about one-third nationally are classified as special education students, and many of the others are below grade level in reading, writing, and mathematics for other reasons. Even though the vast majority of students who enroll in two-year postsecondary technical schools come from high school CTE programs, their postsecondary teachers are not prepared to address their students' learning difficulties in the context of their postsecondary CTE programs.

A system for training and licensing high school and postsecondary CTE teachers that is completely separate from the system and institutions for licensing academic teachers would help. These teachers need industry-recognized credentials for the occupational areas they teach, in addition to pedagogically relevant coursework. National industry associations could establish national criteria for programs that prepare CTE teachers to teach in our high schools, postsecondary technical schools, community colleges, and schools of education.

These prospective teachers also need a relevant licensing test of reading and writing skills. In Massachusetts, instead of continuing to require them to pass the same skills test used for licensing "academic" teachers (which required them to read literary passages among other items and write in response to them), we developed a test called a "Test of Vocational Technical Literacy Skills." Today these prospective teachers take a test whose test items were selected and vetted by members of occupational trades and technical schools in the state. Test takers are asked to read invoices, directions for installing something, and other kinds of texts directly relevant to the trades apt to be taught in vocational/technical programs. This test, in place for a decade, is seen as a fairer test of needed reading and writing skills by prospective teachers who may have no more than a high school education and do not teach discipline-based knowledge to their students.

In sum, CTE teachers need:

1. A separate system of licensure that requires industry-recognized credentials.
2. Pedagogical coursework related to their occupation or trade.
3. A relevant test of their reading, writing, and mathematical skills.

REQUIRE THE SAME ACADEMIC ADMISSION STANDARDS AS OTHER COUNTRIES

It is common knowledge that this country draws most of its teachers from the bottom two-thirds of our college population (most elementary teachers actually come from the bottom third). This was noted in a 2010 McKinsey report,[1] as well as in a 2006 report by the National Center on Education and the Economy titled "Tough Choices or Tough Times." The McKinsey report further noted that high-achieving countries like South Korea, Finland, and Singapore draw those they train as teachers from an application pool consisting of their most academically able high school or college students—the top third. In contrast, only 23 percent of American teachers come from the top third.

McKinsey's report also suggested that the United States could learn from Singapore, which offers large retention bonuses (between $10,000 and $36,000 every few years) for the highly selected teachers already in its schools, or from Finland, which admits fewer than one in ten applicants to its eight teacher training programs—all now located within its university system. A particularly interesting piece of information in the report is the response to a survey asking 1,600 top thirders in their college cohort about their perceptions of teaching and other careers. It found that for those who didn't pick teaching, it was mainly because the profession didn't offer prestige or peer groups with whom they'd enjoy working. Given the prevailing "open door" policy for admission to our education schools, we should perhaps be grateful that as many as 23 percent of U.S. teachers are top thirders.

LEARN FROM CHANGES IN THE BAY STATE'S LICENSING SYSTEM FOR PROSPECTIVE TEACHERS

There were three major deficiencies in the licensure tests we revised in 2000 to 2003 in the Bay State: insufficient input from academic experts on the topics and weights for a discipline-based test for elementary, middle, or high school teachers; indifference to literate cultural knowledge on tests for teachers of foreign languages, performing arts, and other areas in the humanities; and low expectations for what prospective elementary, special education, and early childhood teachers should know about the subjects they teach in a typical school curriculum. In fact, most of the licensure tests we revised for early childhood, elementary, and special education teachers had originally required even less academic knowledge than these prospective teachers had had to demonstrate for college admission or even for graduation from middle school.

Despite the fact that the weaknesses in the licensing regulations and licensure tests were unevenly addressed because of pushback from self-interested groups in the schools or in teacher training programs themselves, academically stronger teachers did emerge from the changes we were able to make in the early 2000s. Let's look at available statistics in each of the areas we sought to strengthen.

One area we sought to strengthen was early childhood and the test for prospective teachers whose license covers preschool to grade 2. For those in Early Childhood programs taking the licensure test addressing the curriculum they are to teach, one may compare the percentages of first-time test takers' pass scores in nine early test administrations (1999 to 2000), before new regulations or new tests were in effect, with the corresponding percentages in the past nine test administrations available. (Numbers and percentages of first-time test takers passing the tests they took are available for each test administration and subject since 1998 at http://www.doe.mass.edu/mtel/results.html.)

The average pass rate for first-time test takers in nine early test administrations was 71 percent. For the last nine test administrations available, the average pass rate was 58 percent. Assuming that these prospective teachers are still from the bottom third of their college cohort (i.e., no change in program admission requirements), it seems that a smaller percentage of those enrolled in this licensure program is passing a more rigorous test despite presumably stronger programs. How many also pass the required test of reading foundations (90) cannot be teased out of the overall percentages of test takers taking that test because three different groups of prospective teachers are required to take it. If students in an Early Childhood program pass both tests, apply for a license in Massachusetts, and teach in its public schools, it is reasonable to conclude that they are an academically stronger group of teachers today, whether they teach preschool, kindergarten, or grade 1 or 2. (Nor is there any reported shortage of prospective Early Childhood teachers for preschool to grade 2.)

A second area we sought to strengthen was the middle school. We cannot compare first-time test takers' pass rates on recent tests with those on any original tests because new licenses and tests were created for this purpose. But we can look at the numbers and pass rates for the Middle School Mathematics/Science and Middle School Humanities tests, both restricted to prospective teachers for grades 5–8. On the Middle School Humanities test, an average of 41 percent of 188 first-time test takers over the seven most recent test administrations passed. A small number of test takers also passed retests. On the Middle School Mathematics/Science test, an average of 38 percent of 193 first-time test takers over the nine most recent test administrations passed. A small number also passed retests on this test, too. So, did we strengthen the middle school? The question can be answered only with another question.

Recall that the original licensing regulations were changed to allow a reduction in the academic load for prospective middle school teachers (and, later, for the second stage of licensure for these teachers), possibly as a way to increase the popularity of these licensure programs. But is it better to have a steadily growing supply of academically competent middle school teachers, even if there are not enough to go around at any one time, or to fill most teaching positions in the middle school with academically incompetent teachers all the time?

We also sought to strengthen the teaching of high school subjects. We eliminated the possibility of a General Science teacher in grades 9–12 and a Social Studies teacher at any grade level. Since then, newly hired teachers have had to be trained in an area of science (e.g., chemistry) or in history or political science as disciplines to teach these subjects. Although there are relatively few test takers for the test in political science/political philosophy, and a relatively low pass rate, NES estimated it at the beginning college level in difficulty, making it among the academically strongest tests of all those now offered in the state. Prospective teachers who have passed that test and later teach in the public schools may be capable of countering the ideological thrust of the newly revised Advanced Placement U.S. History course or the Big History Project promoted by the Bill and Melinda Gates Foundation because the licensure test stresses the philosophical antecedents of the U.S. Constitution.

Figure 12.1 (p. 140) shows the pass rate on all test administrations in 2010 of the revised history test and the new political science/political philosophy test.[2] As can be seen, the number of first-time test takers passing the new test at each administration of the test in 2010 ranges from 10 percent to 54.5 percent of the total of those taking the test for the first time. We do not know what kind of courses they have taken as (most likely) political science or history majors or minors.

It may seem at first that what we did amounts to a relatively small number of more academically competent middle school and high school teachers if those who passed their licensure tests applied for a license, got a teaching position, and stayed in their jobs for at least a few years. Yet, Bay State students made academic gains at all grade levels on a variety of measures. Moreover, they made and kept first place on our national tests (NAEP) and achieved and kept high standing on an international test (TIMSS). Was it just stronger standards or an increasing number of stronger teachers or possibly both?

SOME SPECIFIC CHANGES TO MAKE

It is not clear why governors, state legislators, and school administrators don't demand higher academic admission standards for state-accredited, teacher training institutions or, at the least, stronger mathematics coursework for aspiring elementary teachers. If it is the case, as recent research by economists suggests, that the academic caliber of those who become teachers has declined since 1960, and, as research also suggests, that teacher preparation programs have not strengthened academic requirements for those they admit (or raised the academic bar for admission), there are several courses of action for policy makers to pursue.

1. *Legislators can raise the academic bar for admission to a teacher preparation program.* We cannot expect blood from a turnip. If those who teach in K–6 are on average academically weaker than earlier generations of elementary teachers—and teachers' knowledge of the subject they teach is the only evidence-based characteristic of an effective teacher—then we need to raise the aca-

Test Name	First-Time Test Takers		Test Retakers	
	N	% Pass-ing	N	% Pass-ing

November 2010

History	207	74.4	83	38.6
Political Science/Political Philosophy	9	11.1	6	50.0

September 2010

History	100	68.0	63	20.6
Political Science/Political Philosophy	11	54.5	5	40.0

July 2010

History	257	75.9	89	40.4
Political Science/Political Philosophy	10	40.0	6	0.0

May 2010

History	233	71.7	87	29.9
Political Science/Political Philosophy	10	10.0	8	12.5

March 2010

History	255	76.5	95	32.6
Political Science/Political Philosophy	20	25.0	8	37.5

Figure 12.1. First-Time Test Takers and Test Retakers for the Licensure Tests for History and Political Science/Political Philosophy, March 2010–November 2010. Source: Massachusetts Department of Education website

demic level of those who are permitted to teach. State legislators can do this in several different ways.

    a. They can eliminate undergraduate teacher preparation programs and require all prospective teachers to enroll in postbaccalaureate teacher preparation programs of no more than two years in duration. This would ensure four years of undergraduate coursework in the arts and sciences. Legislators could continue to require an undergraduate major in a subject taught in K–12 for those enrolling directly in a postbaccalaureate preparation program. (For mid-career changers, an academically strong, department-based examination would suffice.)

    b. Legislators can disallow academic credit at the postbaccalaureate level for undergraduate coursework in education.

    c. Legislators can limit admission to teacher preparation programs to only those students in the top two deciles in their high school graduating class.

    d. Legislators can reduce the number of teacher preparation programs in the state to colleges with high general admission standards.

2. *Legislators can mandate licensure tests that require extensive knowledge of the subjects taught at the grade levels covered by the license—and for the entire range of students apt to be at those grade levels.* This is what Massachusetts now does. For example, all prospective teachers for elementary-age children (regular classroom as well as special education teachers) must pass separately scorable subject area tests in the subjects they teach: one in reading instructional knowledge, a second in elementary mathematical knowledge, and a third covering the other major subjects taught in a self-contained classroom in the elementary school (science, children's literature, writing, language, history, and geography).

    Teacher licensing tests can contribute to greater academic quality in teachers under certain conditions:

    a. If licensure tests are strong tests of subject area knowledge, including reading instructional knowledge, as is the foundational reading test now required in Massachusetts, Connecticut, Wisconsin, New Hampshire, and North Carolina.

b. If teacher preparation programs are held accountable for students' passing their licensure tests. This is the case with many occupational licenses. Passing the licensure test is part of the training program a student pays for (e.g., cosmetology). If a student doesn't pass, the program is responsible.

c. If teacher preparation programs are required to submit lists of all students participating in the first year of their program, as well as lists of those who complete their program, in order to ensure that they are accounting for and accountable for all students they enroll.

3. *Legislators can make their state's current educator licensure tests count for far more than they now do without changing them.* Half of those in teacher preparation programs who get licensed in this country never become teachers, the McKinsey report also tells us. We currently award teaching licenses to 100 percent more teachers than we actually need, instead of tailoring supply to demand to some extent. Just passing a bill to reduce drastically the number of those admitted into licensure programs for prospective early childhood and elementary teachers alone would go a long way in upgrading the academic quality of those who become teachers of young children.

4. *State legislators can offer core subject teachers a monetary incentive to take authentic graduate courses in their discipline or in related arts and science coursework rather than content-empty courses in a degree program in education.* This is far more important than they may realize, as the next section suggests.

ABOVE ALL, REQUIRE QUALIFIED CURRICULUM DIRECTORS IN K–12

The strongest step state legislators can take to strengthen the school curriculum is by requiring at least one "discipline-based" supervisor in the central office. Among the requirements for a curriculum supervisor or director in the Bay State's licensing regulations, we added the following options for "directors, department heads, and curriculum specialists in the core academic subjects at the secondary level (5–12)":

a. A master's degree in the arts and sciences in one of the core academic subjects they will supervise, or
b. At least 18 credits of advanced graduate studies in one of the core academic subjects they will supervise. [3]

Why did we do this? We added this qualification after meeting school administrators from across the state on new programs for training school administrators. Once upon a time in large cities, we were told, it was the case that the person serving as a curriculum director often had a Ph.D. in the subject area (especially in science or a foreign language), if not a master's degree in the subject from the arts and sciences. Now, we were told, it was hard to find a curriculum director or even department head in a high school with more than a major in the subject that he or she was now supervising, whether for K–12, 5–12, or 9–12. Worse, many supervisors had multiple subjects to supervise and often didn't have a major in any of them.

Since curriculum directors often evaluate or choose textbooks for the subjects they supervise, help to work out course sequences in the areas under their supervision, help to hire new teachers in the areas under their supervision, and help to evaluate those teachers and student teachers in these areas, a requirement of graduate-level work in one of the subjects they supervised did not seem like too much to expect. All state legislatures could require this qualification for whatever school administrator is in charge of any subject or combination of subjects in the K–12 curriculum. That would start our public school system on the long road to sanity.

NOTES

1. Byron Auguste, Paul Kihn, and Matt Miller, "Closing the Talent Gap: Attracting and Retaining Top Third Graduates to a Career in Teaching," McKinsey and Company, 2010. http://mckinseyonsociety.com/closing-the-talent-gap/.

    2. Massachusetts Tests for Educator Licensure (MTEL), Massachusetts
Department of Elementary and Secondary Education. http://www.doe.mass.
edu/mtel/results.html.
    3. Massachusetts Department of Elementary and Secondary Education,
"603 CMR 7.00: Educator Licensure and Preparation Program Approval."
http://www.mass.gov/courts/docs/lawlib/600-699cmr/603cmr7.pdf.

ABOUT THE AUTHOR

Sandra Stotsky is professor of education emerita, University of Arkansas, and was Senior Associate Commissioner at the Massachusetts Department of Elementary and Secondary Education from 1999-2003. She is the author of several books on curriculum and standards for K–12, and has published many reports and articles on teacher training and teacher licensing tests.